Full Throttle: The Bruce Kessler Story

By Dean Kirkland

Historic photos- Bruce Kessler

Our time with Bruce and his wife. June 8, 2020

(L to R) – Sal Munir, Bruce Kessler, Joan Freeman (wife), Dean Kirkland, Barnaby Brokaw

Sonny, Bruce and Chuck. **Photo -Dean Kirkland**

Table of Contents

Foreword

Sometimes, the universe conspires to connect us with remarkable individuals who change the course of our stories, just as they are about to change their own. When I first met Bruce Kessler, it was for what I thought would be a straightforward interview for a documentary on the legendary Scarab race car. However, as Bruce began to recount his experiences, his tales transcended the confines of mere racing anecdotes. It quickly became evident that his life merited a deeper exploration than our initial project could accommodate. This book was born from that realization—a deeper dive not just into Bruce's professional legacy but into the essence of the man himself.

From the moment I stepped into Bruce's home, his warmth and charisma were palpable. He had a way of storytelling that was utterly captivating, bringing to life the roar of engines and the quiet moments between the noise with equal skill. His anecdotes were punctuated by laughter, his reflections by a wisdom hard-earned over decades of living boldly. I was there to capture the story of a race car driver, but I left with the seeds of this book, eager to share the story of a man who lived with unbridled passion.

This book, "Full Throttle," was meant to be a surprise for Bruce—a token of appreciation for his trust and hospitality, a narrative testament to his multifaceted life. I imagined handing it over to him, watching his reactions as he revisited his past pages, perhaps adding yet another story to his collection. I looked forward to April 10th, 2024, with a mix of anticipation and pride.

However, just as I was putting the final touches on the manuscript, ready to send it to print, I received the heart-wrenching news of Bruce's passing on April 8th, 2024. The news struck a chord deep within me; grief mingled with a profound sense of loss—not just for myself but for all those who would never get to meet him or hear his voice fill a room.

It is with a heavy heart that I dedicate this book to Bruce. While he never got the chance to see it completed, it stands as a tribute to his extraordinary journey through life. Through these pages, I hope to extend his legacy, allowing readers to encounter the man I was fortunate enough to get to know, even if just for a brief time.

Bruce's story is one of triumph, tenacity, and the relentless pursuit of passion, whether behind the wheel, behind the camera, or in the simple act of telling a story. With this book, I say thank you to Bruce, not just for the stories he shared, but for the life he lived so fully. May his tales inspire others as they have inspired this telling.

To Bruce, who raced through life with courage and left tracks on the hearts of all who knew him, this book is for you.

Thank you, Bruce, for everything. Your legacy races on.

Dean Kirkland

The Starting Line

In the world of racing and film, names come and go, leaving behind the dust of memories that either settle into the forgotten corners of history or are polished by the tales of those who remember. My name is Bruce Kessler, and while today's endeavors find me far from the roaring crowds and flashing cameras, my journey through life's twisting tracks and unpredictable scripts has been anything but ordinary.

Born in the heart of Seattle in 1936, my childhood was marked not by the physical exertions of sports, as one might expect from a future racer, but by the silent struggle for breath. Asthma, my constant and unwelcome companion, dictated a life of limitations. The adrenaline shots that momentarily eased my wheezing were a stark reminder of what I couldn't do—until I found my refuge in the roar of engines and the smell of burning rubber. Racing wasn't just a sport to me; it was a declaration of defiance against the constraints of my body.

My cousin, Gene Wolfen, a titan on the sprint car tracks, unknowingly lit the fuse of my racing dreams. His victories and the thunderous applause that followed were intoxicating to a young boy sidelined by his own lungs. In racing, I saw a world where my physical limitations vanished behind the wheel of a machine that responded only to skill, courage, and the will to push harder, faster.

The journey that led me to the sun-drenched roads of California, away from Seattle's damp embrace, was one of necessity. My parents, in their relentless quest for a cure to my ailments, decided that California's promise of sun and mild weather would be my salvation. Little did they know it would also be the birthplace of my racing destiny.

The transition from a mere enthusiast to an active participant in the racing world began with an innocuous family decision: my father purchased a used XK120 for my mother. This sleek Jaguar, with its curves that whispered of speed and freedom, was my ticket into the world I longed to join. I was a hot rodder at heart, a teenager with a thirst for speed and a knack for mechanics, drawn inexorably to the potential nestled within that Jaguar's engine.

My initial foray into racing was met with scepticism at the local drag races. The XK120 and I were outliers, misfits in a world that didn't know how to categorize a production car with the heart of a racer. It was Pappy Petticoat, a name synonymous with kindness and petrol in my young mind, who steered me toward my destiny. His suggestion to enter the Santa Barbara road race was the nudge I needed, a push towards a track that would welcome the Jaguar and me with open arms.

The day I signed up for that race marked the end of my life as I knew it and the beginning of everything that was to come. The waiver, a mere formality for most, symbolized my leap into a world where age and asthma held no sway. Signed by my mother under the watchful eye of Ken Miles, it was my rite of passage. Ken, with his British accent and an air of authority, was the first of many legends I would encounter on my journey. His approval was a badge of honor, a silent acknowledgment that I belonged.

Racing in Santa Barbara wasn't just about the thrill of speed; it was a declaration of independence, a statement to the world, and more importantly, to myself, that I was more than my limitations. Every turn of the track, every gear shift, was a note in a symphony of defiance, a melody that spoke of a life lived on my terms.

This is the story of how a boy with wheezing breaths found his voice in the roar of engines and carved a path through life that was uniquely his. From the rain-soaked streets of Seattle to the sunlit roads of California, from the solitary confines of asthma to the camaraderie of the racetrack, my journey has been one of transformation, of finding freedom in the most unlikely of places.

But, as with any race, the starting line was just the beginning. The tracks I raced, the cars I tamed, and the life I led away from the asphalt—each chapter of my story is a testament to the fact that sometimes, the longest journeys begin with a single lap.

The Early Years and A Passion Ignited

Man, growing up in California in the 1950s, cars were our religion. You couldn't be a kid back then and not have that bug, that need to make your ride your own. We'd chop 'em, channel 'em, drop in new engines, slap on some wild paint. Parents never got it – they'd ask why Detroit didn't just do this stuff themselves. Like, mom, it's not about Detroit, it's about us! It's about making something that screams, "This is mine!"

My pride and joy was this chopped and channeled '47 Mercury convertible. Dark green – not sparkly green, a deep, classy green. Shaved door handles, solenoids rigged up underneath. Interior? White tuck-and-roll, all done by Tony Nancy himself. I mean, this car had the touch of the best – Barris, Nancy, even Von Dutch threw in some pinstriping. That was the dream, to have your car worked on by those guys.

Now, my mom, God bless her, she just didn't understand the appeal. She'd look at that low-slung Merc and say, "Honey, that's beautiful, but how are you going to get girls in that thing?" I'd just grin because, hey, figuring that part out was half the fun, right? You gotta be resourceful when your car has no door handles.

Of course, there was the other car in our garage – my dad's prized XK120 Jaguar. That was a different beast entirely. Brand new, gleaming chrome, all sleek curves. My mom surprised him with it for their anniversary, which totally shocked me because she wasn't really a car person. But that Jag, it got to me, I'll admit. There was something different about it, something powerful and refined. I'd sneak it out sometimes, late at night when they were asleep, just to feel it roar down Pacific Coast Highway. That's when I started to understand that there was more to this car thing than just making them look insane. There was the power, the finesse, the sheer thrill of handling a machine designed for raw performance.

Anyway, all this car obsession, it led me to the shows. The big ones, like the Pan Pacific Automotive Show. Back then, those shows were where you found the real talent – George Barris himself, guys from the hot rod magazines, maybe even a Hollywood insider looking for the next movie car. And wouldn't you know it, my crazy Merc caught a few eyes. People were asking questions, snapping photos, even winning me a couple of trophies. And that's when it hit me: maybe there was more to this than just messing around in the garage.

Next thing you know, the folks from Pan Pacific want MY car in THEIR booth. Me, just some punk kid from LA, right? So I'm there, hanging out by the Merc (trying to look all nonchalant, but failing miserably), and who comes up to me but this skinny, greasy-looking guy with the most intense stare you've ever seen. Turns out, it's Von Dutch! The pinstriping legend!

I'd just assumed the guy was a myth, something the older hot rodders talked about to impress newbies like me. But nope, there he was, checking out my car like it was a priceless painting. We get to talking, and here's the thing: he wasn't some pretentious snob, like you'd expect. He's into the work, the fact I did a bunch of it myself with my buddies. He even starts painting on the booth wall right there in front of me! No stencils, no measurements, just his brush and a can of black paint. The guy creates this whole scene – a crack opening up, a skeletal hand reaching out…it was unbelievable. That moment it clicked for me: this wasn't just tinkering, this was art, you know? Raw, rough-edged, but real art. Looking back, Von Dutch showing up that day, that was like a little prophecy. He'd be popping in and out of my life over the years, always reminding me that beneath the grease and the speed, there was something bigger.

That whole thing – the car show, meeting Von Dutch – it was like a slingshot. Suddenly, I wasn't just some kid with a tricked-out ride, I saw there was a next level. Which, naturally, is when I got myself into a whole heap of trouble.

You see, I figured, alright, I've got the car show thing down, time to try the real deal – racing. Pismo Beach Hill Climb was the first event on my radar. Now, it was a dirt course, meant for sports cars. Phil Hill was there, the legend himself, along with all the big names from the Southern California racing scene.

Here's the thing: I was 16, and I'd never raced seriously before. A few street races, sure, some messing around on dry lakes, but nothing like this. So I roll up in my Merc with my buddies – Chuck, my brain-trust mechanic, and Wally, who loved cars but mostly loved being around cars – and I'm feeling like a million bucks. Until that first practice run.

Turns out, a slammed Merc with no door handles isn't ideal for dirt track racing. I'm taking those corners like I'm back on Sunset, sideways, fishtailing, basically just trying to stay on the damn course. Total disaster. By the time I pull back into the pits, I'm ready to crawl under a rock and never come out. Chuck and Wally, bless 'em, wouldn't let me give up. They're talking strategy – find a guy who knows what he's doing, follow his line, ease up on the gas. Back then, it might as well have been Chinese, but something about their determination started to rub off on me.

Pride, stubbornness, maybe just stupidity – whatever it was, I went back out there. And that's when I got my first real lesson: it's not always about being the fastest, it's about being the smartest. I stuck behind this little MG, watched how it took the turns, and started to actually get the hang of it. Hell, by the time the race started, I was feeling almost cocky. Famous last words, right?

I won that race. Clean and clear, beat Phil Hill in his fancy C-Type Jaguar, the whole nine yards. Suddenly, I'm the star of the show! People are cheering, wanting autographs. It was the craziest rush I'd ever felt. Right after that, the guys from Pan Pacific found me again, asking if they could display my trophies in their booth. Of course, I said yeah, but honestly, I was thinking, "Trophies? Is that all I am now, some sideshow attraction?" It was a weird feeling, that high mixed with something a little hollow.

My buddies, they became my first real pit crew after that. Always there to wrench, to strategize, to remind me that this wasn't just about winning, but about getting better each time. Which was a good thing, because the next big race knocked me right back down to earth.

Santa Barbara – road course, the real deal. And the Merc? Totally outclassed. Ferraris, Maseratis, guys who made me and my chopped convertible look like a joke. And sure enough, I was a joke. Every lap, they were blowing past me like I was going in reverse. Frustration got the better of me – I'm barreling into corners at full tilt, tires screeching. When I finally limp back to the pits, totally dejected, Chuck and Wally aren't yelling, they're just looking at me with this mix of pity and disappointment.

"Bruce," Chuck says, "you gotta slow down. Stop trying to be a hero, and start driving smart." It took a while for that to sink in my thick skull, but eventually, I got it. Being fast wasn't just about guts, it was about brains. Figuring out the corners, finding that sweet spot where you're pushing the limits without becoming a total wreck.

So, I went back out there for the second race. And wouldn't you know it, that's when everything changed. Like, some switch flipped in my brain. I wasn't fighting the car anymore, I was flowing with it. Suddenly, it wasn't about being flashy, it was about being smooth. I even passed a few guys who were making the same mistakes I had earlier! Sure, I didn't win – still a long way off from that level – but ending that race on the podium… well, that feeling was pure. It was proof that maybe I did have what it took, not necessarily to be the best, but to always be better than I was yesterday.

Funny thing about that Santa Barbara race: it wasn't just about learning to drive. See, while I'm sweating it out on the track, the movie business comes knocking.

Turns out, Universal was filming something called "Johnny Dark" starring Tony Curtis. They needed a car to crash through a hangar door, and figured my Merc, with its lead sled looks, would be perfect for the job. So there I am, grease monkey kid from LA, suddenly getting paid 50 bucks (a fortune back then!) to do a stunt for Hollywood. I still don't know if the scene ever made the final cut, but who cares? Chuck, naturally, is beside himself since he's got this dream of being a big-shot cameraman. He's trying to get the perfect shot, whining about how I'm not centered in the frame. I'm telling him to just relax and practice, figuring he'll get his chance someday... and sure enough, the guy ends up a legend, shooting Formula 1 and everything.

Anyway, that little detour gave me a taste for the whole movie scene. I mean, there was something about the energy of a film set that felt familiar, like it was just another version of being in a race paddock. And it made me realize that even if I wasn't the one behind the camera, racing had a place in that world, and that world was a lot bigger than Southern California.

So, I'm coming off this whole Santa Barbara experience – the victories, the lessons, and even the taste of Hollywood – and I'm thinking, "Alright, if these old, stuffy guys can do this racing thing, so can I." I was still a kid, a little cocky, maybe a lot cocky, but there was this new determination in me. I was going to learn how to do this right, and I was going to go all the way with it.

Now, this part of the story, it gets a little fuzzy. See, that's the thing about the early days of motorsport – it wasn't this organized, well-oiled machine like it is today. Things just kinda happened, opportunities popped up out of nowhere. Like, one minute I'm still racing my Merc, and the next, I'm driving something totally different.

It started with these two guys, Jack Arterburn and Maury Carton. Jack was this technical writer, wrote instruction manuals or something boring like that. Maury was the opposite, total academic, a professor type over at UCLA. The thing is, they got the racing bug and bought themselves an MG TC, then figured out they had no clue how to actually drive the thing fast.

I'm working at the local gas station by this point, saving up for whatever my next car project would be, and these guys start showing up regularly. Probably saw me eyeing their MG and finally they ask if maybe, just maybe, I'd like to try driving it. Well, hell yeah, I would! I mean, it wasn't a Ferrari, but it was a real race car, and that's all that mattered at the time.

That MG led me to my next ride. Which, if you can believe it, was even weirder.

Thing is, I'm on my way to Willow Springs for one of its first-ever races – I'd actually done okay there, even beat a guy in a 4.1 Ferrari – and we stop at this little coffee shop along the way. Restroom there was tiny, one door, first come first served. And wouldn't you know it, I beat this older guy, someone my dad's age, to the punch. We end up having this awkward exchange at the door, me all smug about being faster on my feet.

Turns out, that old guy? He was someone important, someone I'd basically insulted without knowing it. While we're getting ready for the race, I wander over to the pit area for Worldwide Motors, a famous racing outfit back then. Wanted to borrow a tool or something, and who do I see but bathroom-door guy! Only now he's sitting there like royalty, and the team owner, Bud Hand, is practically bowing to him.

After I leave, bathroom-door guy starts asking questions about me, the kid who stole his spot in line for the john. Bud and some of the mechanics tell him I'm a local racer making a name for himself, driving this hopped-up MG. Well, long story short, that guy – I still had no idea who he was – liked what he saw in me during that MG race. Even though I crashed out, he was impressed enough with my raw speed and guts that he offered me the chance to drive a car they were building, a way more serious machine than anything I'd ever handled.

That's how I landed in the seat of a Seata Special. Little open-wheel thing, crazy lightweight. And that car, that's when things started getting real. Driving the Seata pushed me like nothing before. It was all about precision, smooth lines, finding those extra milliseconds in a corner. Every time I got behind the wheel, I was improving, learning, starting to be noticed by people who weren't just local hotshots. Which was all part of the plan, right?

Around this time, a guy named Warren Olsen comes into my life. We're talking a whole different breed of cat here. Most racing guys were loud, maybe a bit rough around the edges, always had something to prove. Warren? He was... quiet. Like, wouldn't say three words in a row if he could get away with two. Just this calm, almost mysterious presence. But man, you looked into those eyes, and you knew there was something different about him.

See, Warren was a genius with machines. I'm not just talking about tuning engines, though he was one of the best. I mean, the guy could take a pile of junk and make it race-worthy. We're talking swapping parts from different makes, jury-rigging things together – the kinda stuff that would make a purist cringe, but the damn thing would work. And work well. That's a rare talent.

Warren, he saw something in me, I guess. Didn't come out and say it –that wasn't his style – but he started giving me little jobs at his shop. I was still in high school, thought maybe I'd follow in his footsteps, become a real mechanic. Turned out, I wasn't exactly gifted in that department.

Fact is, I just didn't have the touch. Ask me to take an engine apart, and it'd end up a pile of bolts on the floor. Give me a wrench, and I'm more likely to strip a thread than tighten something correctly. Chuck used to laugh his head off watching me struggle, and even Warren, bless his patient heart, would let out a little sigh before showing me how it was done.

But the thing is, even though I was a disaster with the tools, I soaked up knowledge like a sponge. Hanging around that shop, watching Warren work his magic, talking to him about setups and strategy – that's where I really started to understand the science behind racing. See, I had the guts, maybe even a bit of raw talent, but I was missing the brains of the operation. Warren helped fill that gap.

Then came the real test. He starts talking about Formula 3, something I'd barely heard of back then. These little open-wheelers, they looked like toys to me. And here's Warren, saying that's where I need to go next if I want to be serious about this racing thing. European circuits, top-level drivers… honestly, it felt like a different world.

But here's the thing about Warren – when he did speak, you listened. And I had this gut feeling that he was right, even if it scared the hell out of me. So, once again, I took that leap, trusting that he knew something I didn't.

And wouldn't you know it, he was right again. Formula 3, that's where I cut my teeth, where I went from being some hotshot California kid to a real driver. The competition, the intensity, the whole scene – it was make or break, and I wouldn't be where I am without it. That all started because Warren Olsen saw something in me that maybe I hadn't even seen in myself.

Of course, I stayed true to my roots. I might have been racing in Europe, but it was the hot rod spirit that got me there. The tinkering, the pushing limits, the doing-it-yourself mentality – that never left me. And hey, maybe I wasn't meant to be rebuilding engines in a back-alley garage. But you better believe I always made damn sure I had the best mechanics in my corner, guys who shared that same passion for making machines do the impossible.

Back at Warren's shop, things were booming. That second garage – right smack in the old car wash where San Vincente meets up with La Cienega – meant we had space for more projects, more mechanics…and more characters hanging around. "Staff" might be too fancy a word, honestly. We were all just kids, gearheads and dreamers, more interested in engines than college.

Take Sonny Balcain (real name Raul). Sharp as a tack, but school wasn't his thing. His dad, big shot Air Force general, realized his kid was too far ahead of the curve to waste his time on textbooks. Turns out the guy was right, but that didn't make Sonny easy to work with. He'd pop up at the shop, full of ideas, but also, let's just say...difficult. Sonny's another story for another day, but you'll get to hear from the man himself later on, I'm sure.

My pal Wally Green, bless his heart, was another fixture by then. Never the best with a wrench, but his enthusiasm made up for his lack of mechanical skill. If you needed something swept, painted, or just fetched, Wally was your guy. Then along comes Lance Reventlow, fresh outta that fancy reform school in Arizona, rolling up in a freaking 300 SL Gullwing. And listen, this is mid-50s, okay? You cruise that thing down Beverly Hills back then, people were literally running into the street, asking, "What the hell is that?" We'd joke around, tell 'em it was a Goldberg, made in Israel, and they'd be like, "Woah, sweet ride!" Shows you how much things have changed, how unique that car was for the time.

So yeah, Lance instantly becomes part of the scene. And like I said, he wasn't the shy type. He'd come around the shop, throwing his weight about – mostly because of his family's money, let's be real – but there was also something else there. A desire to be more than just some rich kid, a real hunger to be part of the racing world.

One day, he picks me up from the shop for lunch. We're in his 300 SL, him behind the wheel, which, knowing Lance, was probably a mistake. We're coming up on Burton Way in Beverly Hills. It's a little sloped there, and there'd been some rain, so the street's a bit wet. Suddenly, car in front of us slams on the brakes. Lance stops, there's the tiniest skid...and we tap the guy. Like, barely even a bump. No serious damage at all.

But Lance, he gets out, looks at this dent the size of a fist on his precious Mercedes (which, let's be real, he probably got from his family fortune), and declares the car totaled. "Forget this," he says, "let's go down to the dealership, pick up all the racing gear – the seats, the roll cage, the whole setup – and you'll race the car for me."

Now, I'm no dummy, even if I was a bit of a hothead back then. "Lance," I tell him, "these Gullwings, great looking machines, but they're not built for the track. Way too heavy, the handling's all wrong. You'd need a whole custom setup, spend a fortune, and even then..." But he's not listening, already fired up, "No, this is what I want to do! You're my driver, right?" Alright then, who am I to argue with the guy who's signs the checks? Besides, maybe there's something to this crazy idea...

So, off we go to the Mercedes-Benz dealership, over to their parts department. This older guy's there, Bill Pig was his name – yeah, really. Turns out, he's this huge Mercedes collector, owns several 300 SLs himself, knew his stuff. Lance walks up, bold as brass, tells him he wants every racing part they make for his car. The parts guy looks confused, and then Bill Pig, who's been listening in, asks if Lance is planning on racing. Lance says no, points straight at me, says Bruce here is going to race it.

The look on Bill Pig's face, priceless. He says something like, "Hold on a second, be right back," and disappears into the manager's office. We can only imagine the conversation, but they call us in, and the manager looks from Lance to me. "So, Bruce," he says, "you're going to drive this car?" Lance confirms it, and that's when things get crazy.

The manager lays out this proposition...and I swear to you, nothing like this could ever happen today. He says he's gonna send us up to Oakland, to this Alfa Romeo dealer – guy's name escapes me right now, shame, 'cause he's part of the story. Anyway, this guy's got a massive warehouse where they store all the imported cars back then, before things got streamlined like they are now. And apparently, there's like 1200 silver 300 SLs sitting there, just waiting for buyers. Thing is, back then there was only one Mercedes dealer for all of Southern California, up near Sunset and, uh...La Brea, I want to say.

So the manager tells us to go find a specific car, even gives us the VIN number. But here's the kicker: take a magnet, he says. The one he wants it won't stick to the body. "What, they're steel!" I say. He just gives me this look, says, "Trust me, and look very closely at the back window. It isn't glass." We're baffled, but hey, sounded like an adventure, so why not? Besides, what's the worse that can happen? We're young, dumb, and think we're immortal, right?

Lance and I, we hop a plane up to Oakland, find this Alfa guy (damn, I wish I could remember his name, important guy in the scene at the time), and there's this whole sea of silver Mercedes, other brands too, just row after row of 'em. I follow the instructions, find the one where the magnet doesn't work, the one with the weird plastic back window and...wouldn't you know it, underneath the paint it's a full-on factory lightweight race car! Probably smuggled in for some rich guy who then backed out.

Now, driving that thing back to LA, that was a different beast than Lance's regular 300 SL. This thing was raw, tuned up, a handful to control. The lightweight body, the stripped-down interior...it felt like a purebred racehorse compared to Lance's pampered show pony. We get it back, and here's where things get even weirder. They paint it the same color as my Cooper, which was sort of this blue I called "Bruce Blue." That color, with the white stripe, it ended up being the paint scheme for the Scarabs later on, funny how things work out.

So now we've got two 300 SLs on the team, the regular one and this hidden lightweight special. We'd take the race car out – they still had Lance's original one too – and I'd get sent to some track with a German mechanic, even though Warren and the guys were around. It's not that they didn't trust Warren, but I think these big European manufacturers wanted their own guys there, part of the show. They let Lance drive it once, down at Torrey Pines, and the guy promptly bashes in the fender. I still win the race, but everyone knows Lance did it, which secretly made me chuckle a bit, gotta admit.

He gets this itch to start racing himself. "Bruce, let me try it!" he'd say. We're talking about a high-strung race car, not some street machine. But what the hell, it was a different time. We'd go out to Riverside or Pomona, somewhere local, and let him take a few laps, just to get the feel for it. He wasn't terrible, but he wasn't ready for primetime either. That's when Warren – who by now had become tight with Lance – figures we can get Lance the Cooper dealership. I was getting some attention for driving the 500s, but no one wanted Coopers back then, so it was a win-win. So Lance takes over, gets himself one of those little 1100 center-seaters. Good car to start with, decent handling, not too much power to get you in trouble. At least, not TOO much trouble.

Now, here's a funny little story about that car. I mentioned Von Dutch before, right? Well, we get him to come down to the shop and stripe Lance's Cooper, told him to do whatever he wants. The car was silver, and what does the crazy guy do? Starts up near the driver's seat and paints this massive spider web all the way down to the nose. Then he draws this huge spider dangling in the web, and the spider's holding this little girl clutching a doll. It was insane, a whole damn art piece on the side of a car! Naturally, Lance loves it, because he's always gotta be the center of attention.

We decide to take it to Elkhart Lake for Lance to race. One look at that thing, and the track officials freak out. Made us tape over the entire front end, all that beautiful artwork covered up! Wouldn't even let him drive. That was sports car racing for you back then, a bunch of stuffy old guys scared of a little creativity, more concerned about their rules than the spirit of the thing. Made me appreciate the hot rod mentality even more – less rules, more guts.

Anyway, that's how Lance got his start, in that crazy spiderweb Cooper, and from there it was onto Formula cars, bigger races, bigger sponsors, and the whole circus that followed him through his career. Guy had talent, no doubt, but also this hunger that you couldn't teach. Sometimes it worked in his favor, sometimes it bit him in the...well, you know.

While Lance was getting his feet wet, I was still tearing up those Formula 3 tracks in Europe. Warren had gotten me hooked up with the best team, the best cars, and I was making a name for myself. I mean, I'd always been confident, but those wins, they solidified something in me. Knew I could go all the way, if I kept my focus.

Thing is, even with the success in Europe, my heart was still back in California. I missed the hot rod scene, the camaraderie of guys like Warren and Wally, that feeling of building something from scratch. And then, out of the blue, comes this opportunity with the Scarabs.

Now, Warren, being the genius he was, had this idea brewing for a while. Build an American-made sports car that could beat those snooty Europeans at their own game. Not just some cobbled-together special, but a real, purpose-built race machine. Lance, with his family connections, could potentially get the funding. And I was the driver, the hotshot Californian who could prove this American dream on wheels wasn't just some fantasy.

We start building these cars...well, Warren and his crew build them, I mostly provide the enthusiasm and maybe hold a wrench now and then to look like I'm helping. But watching them take shape was something else. Hand-built steel frames, lightweight bodywork, and the heart of those machines...American V8s shoehorned in. A Chevy small-block at first, then some bigger, meaner engines. They weren't glamorous, those engines, but they had tons of potential, and Warren knew how to unlock it.

The first time I got behind the wheel of a Scarab...damn, that was a moment. Felt different from anything I'd driven before. Lighter, more responsive, like it was an extension of myself, instead of something I was trying to wrangle. Warren had done his magic, no question.

But the magic wasn't just in the car. It was in the whole scene. We're racing at tracks across the country, and yeah, we're winning our fair share of races. But we're also causing a stir. These big European teams, they look at us at first like we're some kind of joke – hot rodders with too much money on our hands. Remember, they're used to being the top dogs, seeing Americans as good for drag strips and ovals, but not real road racing.

Little by little, though, that changes. They start to see that we're serious. That Scarab blue starts showing up in the winner's circle more and more often. And even if we weren't dominating every single race, we were pushing the limits, proving that Americans could play this game just as well as anyone.

The whole Scarab era, it was a wild ride. It wasn't just about winning trophies (though those were nice). It was about shaking things up, about making people see that this sport, this passion, wasn't just some European club anymore. We were brash, we were raw, we made mistakes...but damn it, we were fast. It was like all that California hot rod spirit, the do-it-yourself attitude, was finally getting its due on the international stage.

There were setbacks, of course. Cars broke down, I made some stupid mistakes on the track. We even lost people – Richie Ginther, one of the best damn drivers out there, killed while testing one of the Formula 1 Scarabs. That hurt, hit the whole team hard. Made us question whether the risk was worth it. But in the end, that's what racing is, right? You push yourself to the edge, and sometimes you go too far. Doesn't mean you stop. You learn, you grow, and you try again.

The Scarabs, they didn't take over the world. Corporate politics, some bad luck, it all kind of fizzled out. But the legacy, that's the important thing. We proved something. We showed a bunch of Europeans that Americans weren't just good at drag racing and ovals – we could build a damn fine sports car and go toe-to-toe with the best.

And for me, personally? It was the next level. Driving those Scarabs gave me the skills and the confidence I needed to move on to the real big leagues – Formula One. Without Warren, without Lance, without that crazy, ambitious project...well, who knows where I would've ended up. Probably still a mechanic back at Warren's, telling stories about how I ALMOST made it big. But because a bunch of us decided to dream a little crazy, I had that shot. And even if I never won a World Championship, I got to drive against the absolute best on some of the most iconic tracks on the planet. That's a win in my book, and none of it would have been possible without those wild early days, building cars and causing trouble back in California.

The Audacity of Von Dutch

Things were always a bit of a whirlwind in those days. Take Elkhart Lake, the time they made us tape up that crazy masterpiece on Lance's Cooper. See, Von Dutch, that wild artist, he'd painted this massive spider web on the car, complete with a spider and a little girl doll. Lance loved it, of course – always had to stand out. But those track officials, they freaked. Wouldn't even let Lance drive with a work of art like that on display. Just another example of those stuffy old guys running the show, scared of a little creativity. Made me appreciate the hot rod spirit even more – less concerned with rules, more about pushing the limits.

Things were moving fast for me around that time, though. Suddenly, I was getting offers to drive sprint cars, maybe even try out for Indy. Wasn't my thing, honestly. But at Warren's shop, we had Cal Neide working for us then. Great guy, Indy driver, even though he'd been injured and was kinda at the end of his career. They also had this guy, Al Sherman, brilliant sprint car builder.

Al builds this one car, a stretched-out midget with a supercharged Offy engine on the front – a real monster. I take it down to Phoenix, and that thing, let me tell you, it could lift the front wheels clean off the ground coming out of a corner! Al was a genius, no doubt about it. He was part of Warren's team by then, but I just didn't see myself going that direction. My heart was set on sports cars, maybe even making the jump to Europe someday. Back then, that was a big dream – not many Americans did that. Phil Hill, sure, and Cunningham's team, but it was still pretty rare.

Right around then, out of the blue, I get a call from this gentleman named Joe Lubin. Very polite, tells me he works with David Brown – that's Aston Martin, in case you didn't know. Joe says David Brown's offered to send me one of his race cars to drive, a DBR3, or maybe it was a DB3, one of those fancy Astons. That was a major break, let me tell you.

One of the funny things I remember about it is we take the car out to Willow Springs for testing, along with a British mechanic. I'm hammering around the track, getting a feel for the Aston, and coming out of the last corner...suddenly the engine's just idling. I pull into the pits, and everyone's asking, "What's wrong, what happened?" I look down, reach under the dash, and I'd clean snapped the gas pedal right off! "Well," I told 'em, "can't say I didn't have my foot in it!" By then, I knew Willow Springs pretty damn well, even outside of my own racing. Always used it for testing.

There was this one time...see, Ernie McAfee, great driver, I even worked for him on and off...Ernie gets me into this Kurtis, might have been McGurk's car, and we're up at Willow Springs. He starts telling me, "You know, Bruce, you can just toss that thing sideways into the first corner, don't even need to brake." I'm looking at him like he's crazy. That sounded like a recipe for disaster. But I nod along, like, "Yeah, sure Ernie."

So, I'm out there in the car, going faster and faster. Come around to that first corner, I'm a bit hot, drift up onto the marbles, and the damn thing starts spinning. Helmet visor's down, eyes shut tight, got a death grip on the wheel...and then I open my eyes, and all I see is this gray-ish blur. "Oh God," I think, "I'm dead. Mom and Dad are gonna kill me. Ernie's gonna be furious, and Mr. McGurk's probably gonna have my hide for wrecking his car."

Next thing you know, I look down and see my own shirt. "Oh shit, I'm alive!" It turns out I'd spun so fast my visor was full of dust. I got the car sorted, sheepishly drove back to the pits, ready to face the music – but the Kurtis was just fine. Ernie...well, he just grinned at me. Great guy, a bit mischievous, but that's racing for you.

Mexican Mayhem

Let's talk about the Mexican Road Race back in '54. Ernie's the one who got me that gig with Rubirosa. Porfirio Rubirosa...now there's a name from the past. The tabloids called him the greatest lover of all time, married all these rich ladies. Hated Lance's guts, because he'd been married to Lance's mother at one point. Anyway, Ernie says to me, "I want you to drive the parts car down to Mexico." Back then, you had to drive your support vehicles way ahead of, or behind, the race itself.

Ernie hooks me up with Zsa Zsa Gabor's new Cadillac to use, tells me to be careful, because, well, it's her car. I picked a buddy of mine, Phil Seberg, big car nut, to come along for the ride. Turns out, we end up in this town, Tuxtla Gutierrez, where the race started. They've also got all those guys from Pikes Peak – the Unser family – down there, more racers than beds to go around.

So, they stick us all in this one hotel, a big ballroom with a bunch of cots. Me, the Unsers, the whole crew, it was a scene. Then, one night, the cops show up, roust us all out of bed. Seems someone stole parts off their police car. We're all standing there, clueless, and one of the Unsers, might have been the dad, steps forward and assures the cops they'll make it right. Turns out, the local police cruiser was the same type of car the Unsers were racing, so they'd pinched the parts they needed! You can check with the Unsers about that one, it's a true story.

That whole Mexican trip...let me tell you, they didn't have a lot of crowd control down there. People would just wander out onto the track, try to touch the cars as they were racing by. It was insanity. Just outside of Tuxtla, there was this drop-off bridge, not a long one, with a couple of planks to keep you level. Then, on the other side, a hill heading up, and a little cafe overlooking the whole thing.

Phil and I, we'd go up there, get coffee, and watch the practice runs. One morning, here comes a school bus, pulls up and stops right at the bridge. At that exact moment, Bill Vukovic comes barreling through in a factory Ford, loses control, just barely clips the bus, slams on the brakes, jumps out, and starts yelling, "Is anyone hurt? Is everyone okay?" The kids are all freaking out, but of course, no one got hurt. Suddenly, everyone's screaming "Bill Vukovic!" wanting autographs.

Now there's a lesson for you: even when you think you've messed up big time, sometimes you just gotta own it. Vukovich turned a potential disaster into a PR opportunity. Ever since then, whenever I find myself in a tight spot, I think, "What would Bill Vukovich do?" Probably not the safest advice, but it's served me well from time to time.

That Mexican adventure, it led to some other interesting opportunities. Not long after, I end up driving in Nassau. Remember those Speed Weeks they used to have down there? Well, I'm racing this little Austin-Healey, one of the ones imported by Briggs Cunningham. It was a fun car, but those Healeys had this nasty habit of the front suspension collapsing. I'm out there in practice, and sure enough, the whole thing gives way. I'm lucky I wasn't going too fast, but the car's a mess.

Word gets around the paddock, and this older gentleman approaches me. Turns out, he's got a Jaguar XK 120 in his garage, and offers to let me race it. Now, that was a serious piece of machinery. I jump in, don't even have time for a real practice session, but I manage to qualify the thing.

Race day comes, and I'm feeling pretty good, all things considered. But wouldn't you know it, just as the flag's about to drop, the Jag's clutch explodes. Talk about bad luck! I don't even get to start the race. But that's how it goes sometimes, you know? You can win one day, and the next, your car falls apart before you even get off the line.

That whole Nassau experience, it taught me something important: always be ready to adapt. Things rarely go according to plan in this business. Whether it's your car failing, or getting a last-minute offer, you gotta be able to roll with the punches and make the most of the situation.

Speaking of making the most of things, there was this time I'm down in Mexico again, racing a Porsche this time. We're doing well, but then the engine starts to overheat. Now, this car had been modified, so the normal water filler cap was gone. We pull into the pits, and the only way to add water is through this tiny little hole, maybe an inch wide. Takes forever, meanwhile, we're losing position fast.

Finally, we get enough water in, get back on the track, but by then, we're way down the order. So, I figure, what the hell, might as well just go for it. I start pushing that Porsche harder than I ever have, taking risks I probably shouldn't. And you know what? We start making up places. By the end of the race, not only did we make up for lost time, but we actually finished on the podium! Goes to show you, sometimes a little desperation can lead to surprising results.

Of course, there were days when even desperation and the best intentions weren't enough. I remember one race, must have been at Riverside or somewhere, I'm driving another one of those Coopers with the Offy engine. Those things were notoriously unreliable, always blowing up. Well, this time, I'm doing well, running with the leaders, and sure enough, the engine lets go. Big cloud of smoke, oil all over the track...race over.

I pull into the pits, fuming. And just then, I see Stirling Moss walking by. Now, Moss was the top driver of his day, a legend. So, I can't resist. I yell out, "Hey Stirling! Want to buy a cheap Offy?" He doesn't even break stride, just gives me this look and keeps walking. Talk about adding insult to injury! But I guess even when you're at your lowest, a little humor can help ease the sting.

All these stories, all these adventures, they shaped me as a driver. Those early years, it wasn't just about winning races, though that was always the goal. It was about figuring things out as you went, learning to adapt on the fly, pushing yourself and your machines to the limit. And let me tell you, sometimes those limits got pushed further than anyone thought was possible. It was a wild ride, and I wouldn't trade it for anything.

Let me tell you about that Mexican Road Race mess. See, it all ended for me down in a place called Nombre de Dios – if I'm getting that right, my Spanish was never the best. Anyway, we were supposed to be following the main race cars, part of the support crew and all that. I was driving Zsa Zsa Gabor's Cadillac – yeah, Ernie hooked me up with that gig – and right behind me was this Ford factory team car with a guy named Johnny Glue at the wheel.

We were all hauling ass, probably pushing 80, 90 miles an hour, when suddenly this whole group of Mexican soldiers goes marching across the road right in front of us. Johnny slams on the brakes, I hit mine, and – bam! – I plow into the back of his Ford. Those soldiers scatter like quail, then they're laughing, like the whole thing was a big joke.

Well, I get out, fuming, and I give one of 'em a good shove – not my proudest moment, but hey, I was young and hotheaded. Next thing you know, they're hauling me and Phil Seberg off to jail in Nombre de Dios. Yep, that was the end of my road trip, and the end of Zsa Zsa's Cadillac too, I might add. Porfirio Rubirosa was a good guy about it, considering, but let's just say that was my one and only adventure with that crew.

Anyways, during that same Mexican trip, Phil Hill ends up winning the whole damn thing. Jack McAfee, great driver, he goes off the road and his co-driver – Robinson, I think his name was – gets killed. Hit Jack hard, I think. They ended up canceling the race after that, which was probably for the best. See, nobody knows the exact count, but a whole lot of spectators died down there. They'd crowd right onto the track, try to touch the cars as they went by. Madness, the whole thing.

So, yeah, that was one hell of a trip. Made me miss those clean California tracks, I'll tell you that much. Speaking of which, there was this time I was back home, must've been '56…let's see, yeah, because Lance had just finished his new house on Davies Drive. Anyway, a big decision was made around then: I was ready for a two-liter car. John Von Neumann, he had a Ferrari Testarossa, and we worked out a deal, my parents involved and everything, where it was gonna get sold to this fella Chester Flynn, big shot at General Motors, real nice guy, up in New York City.

Now, here's the thing: when we took the car back East, I also ended up racing it at Paramount Ranch. And wouldn't you know it, I clipped a tree during the race. Not a write-off, nothing like that, but enough to knock me out of the running. And back then…well, let's just say I was enjoying myself a bit too much. Not before a race, mind you, but during the week, yeah, I was hitting the bottle pretty hard. Only 20 years old, and already drinking like I'd been doing it my whole life.

Used to go to this place, the Luau on Rodeo Drive, all the time. Well, after that Paramount Ranch mess, I head back to Lance's place, and his new house had this jacuzzi that spilled right into one of the rooms. I'm soaking in there, just me and my swim trunks, when Natalie Wood walks in. She looks at me, real serious, and says, "Bruce, if you keep drinking like that, you're going to kill yourself."

That hit me hard. The way she said it, I don't know, it just made me think. And right then and there, before I even turned 21, I quit drinking. Cold turkey. Never looked back. That was one turning point, for sure.

So, we go back East, and this whole other chapter starts. See, the SCCA, they ran the sports car races out there and obviously knew who I was. Sometimes they'd let me race, sometimes not, depending on the rules and whatnot. But guys like John Fitch, they vouched for me. Said, "Nah, this kid knows his stuff, we've raced against him in California, he's alright."

Turns out, I'm gonna be driving for this guy Canetti, and they decide it's okay for me to race, but I need to go through driver's school first. It's still early in the year, race season kicks off in May, and I'm hanging around my dad's office – he had a place back East – when I decide to check out this bookstore called Gordon's. They always had this sports car section in the back, all the magazines and books…I'd spend hours in there.

Well, one day, I'm browsing, and there's this bulletin board with stuff pinned to it. I overhear these two guys, older fellas in sports coats and slacks – the whole East Coast look, while I'm still rocking my jeans and cowboy boots – and they're talking about some Formula 3 car that's for sale. Figuring out what kind of transmission it had, all those technical details. So, I'm reading my books, minding my own business, when I turn around and go, "Yeah, those use motorcycle transmissions."

They stare, trying to figure out if I'm messing with them. Ask a few more questions, and I keep answering, like it's no big deal. Finally, one of them goes, "You a mechanic or something?" I shake my head, and just tell them, "Nah, I'm just the Formula 3 champion back in California." They look at each other, don't know if they believe me. I mean, here's this 20-year-old kid in Levi's, could have been any bum off the street for all they knew.

They finally ask what I'm even doing back East, and I tell them I'm driving for Canetti, that Ferrari guy. They nearly fall over. Turns out, they're all about sports cars too, just your weekend enthusiast types with their MGs and Triumphs. Wouldn't you know it, they end up inviting me to this club gathering they're having. I figure, why not? Made some good friends that night, and hey, for a bunch of guys who thought touching a Ferrari was the pinnacle of existence, taking them to Lime Rock for my first race with that Testarossa? Let's just say they were over the moon.

But back to that driver's school… that was a whole other mess. See, they made it a condition for me racing with the SCCA, and I show up, this kid from California with my jeans and attitude, amidst all these guys in their fancy driving suits and whatnot. Standing there listening to Bill Proctor – Procter & Gamble guy, had himself a nice Maserati, but let's just say his driving skills weren't quite matching his bank account – and he's going on about race theory. Telling everyone, "Here's a secret, I always go into corners slower so I can come out a little faster," and I'm smirking at the back, muttering loud enough for everyone to hear, "I'll be sure to make a note of that." You should have seen the looks I got!

Of course, I had to keep my mouth shut for the rest of the day, couldn't even show them what I could do, 'cause I didn't have a car to practice with. But the SCCA guys, with Fitch and others backing me up, they finally relented.

Now, come that first race at Lime Rock, Lance flies out with the Ferrari, the guys I met at the bookstore are hyped, and it's my first time racing against a whole new crowd. Well, tucked into the under two-liter class with me is none other than the official Jaguar team, owned by Briggs Cunningham himself. I didn't know much about big-name racers then, but Lance sure did. He warns me, "Take it easy, Bruce, don't show them how fast you really are."

Problem was, we were on a track built for cars like mine, and there was Bob Holbert, another hotshot driver at the time, to contend with. If I beat him, I'd be up against the bigger guns in the main race. So, Lance keeps telling me, "Relax, hold back," but I always lead from the first lap. Well, Holbert gets ahead of me at the start, but the race is short, and I only have a few laps to pass him. He's got a Porsche 550, and between the two of us pushing each other, we shatter those lap time records. That's when Cunningham and the Jaguar crew get all twitchy – they realize, hey, this is the perfect track for those little two-liters, not so much their big, heavy cars.

So yeah, I end up in the main race, and here's where things get crazy. They start me at the back of the pack, and I'm thinking, "What in the hell am I gonna do? How do I get through this?" Turns out, they put the top three finishers from the two-liter race in the back, and one of them was Proctor in his Maserati that moved about as fast as a turtle.

Race starts, and it only takes me a few laps to figure out my strategy. There's Proctor, chugging along, acting like he owns the whole track, and up ahead are those two D-Type Jags driven by Hansgen and Fitch. Well, Proctor slows everyone down coming into the first corner, and I see my chance. I squeeze through on the inside, force Proctor wide, and poof! I'm in the lead, with only a lap or two to spare. Now I'm scrambling, trying to figure out if I can hold these guys off…

Turns out, Fitch and Hansgen had swapped places without me even realizing it, and by the final lap, Hansgen's right on my tail. Fitch is swarming me too, and we're going full tilt. Come out of the last corner, onto the straightaway, and all three of us are neck and neck. Hansgen inches ahead – no surprise, that D-Type had the power – and Fitch is about to swallow me whole. We cross the finish line so close, it was the tightest finish they'd ever seen.

Now, back in California, that kind of race wouldn't have made much of a splash. Just a good, hard race. But this was the East Coast, in front of the New York Times, Denise McCluggage… overnight, I'm the talk of the racing world. Sports Illustrated starts calling me "Daring Young Bruce Kessler," and all my friends back at the bookstore can't believe their buddy Bruce is suddenly famous.

Best part? Frank Blunk, the New York Times reporter, comes up to me after, everyone's crowding around, and he asks, "Where did you ever learn to drive like that?" Without even thinking, I say, "Well, everyone in California drives like that." That line made it into papers all over, probably the most famous thing I ever said.

And that, folks, is how a hothead kid from California ended up on top of the East Coast racing scene. Of course, I was promised a ride with Ferrari soon after, but that got all mixed up, and I ended up driving for Porsche instead. But that, as they say, is a whole different story.

Lime Rock

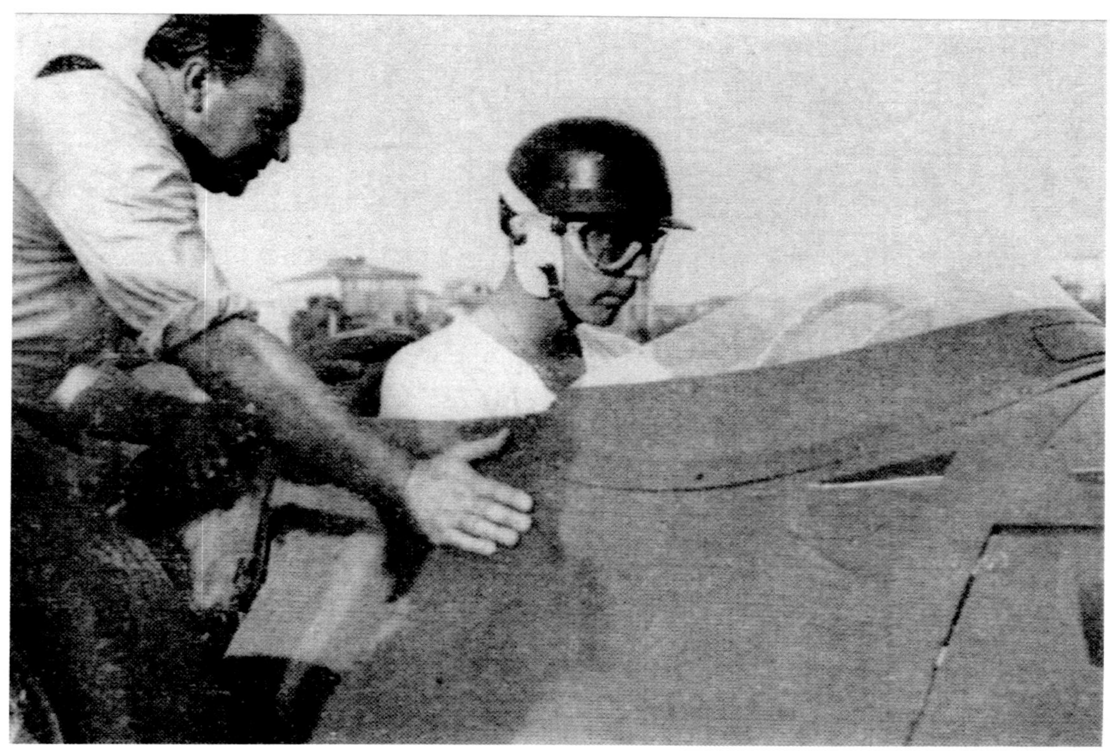

You know, that first time at Lime Rock, I was green as grass. Just 21, and fresh off that California sun. Lance Reventlow – that crazy rascal – shows up, and wouldn't you know, first day of practice they single me out. Call me up to the official stand after the driver's meeting. Lance tags along, of course.

We're standing there, me and him, a couple of kids in our jeans, looking up at this stuffed shirt running the show. Mr. Formal-Pants says, "Mr. Kessler..." – I swear he dragged my name out like I was some kinda criminal – "...this here's Mr. Jones. Corner marshal up on that tricky bend 'round turn two and a half. He's got something for ya."

Jones gives me a real once-over. "Mr. Kessler," he grumbles, "Saw you shifting in that bend. Explain yourself."

I figure, what the heck. "Yeah, topped out at 7,000, just the usual upshift."

Mr. Jones shakes his head, looks at me like I might be the dumbest thing on four wheels. "Hope you know what you're doing, son. Dangerous business."

That's when Lance, God bless him, steps in front of me. "Listen, Mr. Jones. If this kid didn't know his stuff, he'd be waving that flag and you'd be behind the wheel of that Ferrari."

Now, I don't think I've ever told anyone that story before. That night, Lance and I hit the Lime Rock Inn, and the whole place is buzzing. They're arguing over some hotshot driver, this California kid. Lance and I, being the modest young gentlemen we were, tried to explain that this kid wasn't all that. They weren't having any of it! Kept going on and on...shoulda seen him out there today...bla bla bla.

Well, let's just say it got a whole lot funnier when they realized who they were arguing with. Good times, man, good times. That Ferrari I was driving, a 500 TRC, that baby was a dream. Later, it went on to Pete Lovely, and he won the inaugural Laguna Seca with it. Great guy, Pete.

That Lime Rock weekend set things in motion. Other races, other wins...and before you know it, Ferrari wants me for Le Mans. 1957, mind you. But they go quiet, no word for weeks. I figure, that's that. Then, out of the blue, Porsche calls. Wants me to drive one of theirs. American team, me and another kid. Perfect for publicity, they figure. Turns out John Fitch was supposed to be their man, but something came up. John recommends me, and boom, I'm in.

Meanwhile, Lance, he's got himself a Formula 2 car. Plan was always to go over to Europe. He and his buddy Warren are using this old '36 Bentley his mom bought (swanky, huh?) as a tow car. I let him know I'm Europe-bound too, and I'll never forget...I step off the plane in Paris, first trip there, and this guy in a cowboy hat barrels over, screaming "Monsieur Kessler! The great American racer!"

Takes me a minute to realize it's Hans Tonner, this writer guy. Lance and Warren put him up to it, the jokers. They're all doubled over laughing. That was my welcome to Europe.

That same night, Lance tells me he's got dates lined up, one for each of us. "Don't worry, don't worry," he insists, but I'm thinking, come on, where's mine? We're bouncing from place to place, him and his lady friend in tow, until we end up...well, let's just say the sign outside wasn't in English. Turns out, it's a drag club.

I give them a look, like "Okay guys, very funny," but they swear it's all real. So, in we go. They've got this whole show, and at the end, out comes this stunning French blonde, Coke Senelle. Doesn't strip, just sings, but man, she had a voice. After her set, she sits right down at our table. Starts showering me with compliments about what a great racer I am...I'm starting to think my luck has changed, you know? Then I look down, and well...let's just say Coke, she was a master of her craft. Lance and Warren nearly lost it before they could stop things from getting too interesting. Coke was famous, turns out. Tourists would flock to see her sunbathe topless. Magazines, the whole nine yards. That was my first night in Paris, folks.

On to Le Mans, and boy, that was a mixed bag. I'm 21 years old, driving the iconic 24-hours in a Porsche 550 RS. Talk about pressure! My teammate was an older guy, Ed Hugus. A gentleman, good driver, but let's just say, not the most aggressive type. We're a few hours in, and I figure it's my turn to take the wheel. The plan was always for me to do the night shift.

I'm all strapped in, ready to go, when Hugus comes out of the pits. Seems he figured he was good for a few more laps, forgot all about our plan. Well, rules are rules. I end up waiting two extra hours before I get my turn as a result. Now, here's the problem: those two hours were the golden hours at Le Mans. Dusk, turning into night, that's when you REALLY see who's who. I lost that edge, and it cost us.

We still finished, mind you. Seventh overall, first in our class...but it's one of those "what if" moments, you know? Could've been higher up that podium with the right timing. But hey, no regrets. Racing, it's like that. One bad shift, one wrong decision, and bam, the whole landscape changes.

Still, Le Mans was a hell of a ride. The crowds, the noise, that energy...nothing like it on earth. And the track itself – a beast. The Mulsanne Straight, man...you just floor it and pray. Flat out for miles in the dark, headlights barely cutting through. It's enough to put the fear of God in you. Well, in me at least! Some fellas, they seemed to thrive on it.

Take Mike Hawthorn. Ran for Ferrari, British guy. Won Le Mans that year. Absolute madman behind the wheel, but a charmer off the track. Him and Luigi Musso, they were the duo to beat. We used to hang out in the evenings, share stories. Hawthorn always had a bottle of scotch tucked away somewhere. I learned a lot from those guys, even though we were rivals.

Funny thing...a few weeks after Le Mans, I'm out running errands, just driving around LA. Look up, and who do I see tooling around in a gorgeous Ferrari? Hawthorn himself. Seems he'd come over to California special. Stops me, right there in the middle of Sunset Boulevard. Traffic pile-up didn't bother him a bit. Rolls down his window, gives me that wide grin of his.

"Well, Kessler," he says, all casual, "Fancy seeing you here. You drive like this out in California?"

I kinda stammer, try to explain I was just on my way to grab a sandwich or something. He laughs, pats me on the shoulder. "Good to see you, lad. Don't get too comfortable in those street clothes, though. You belong on the track."

Tell you what, that gave me a kick. Hawthorn, winner of Le Mans, telling little old me to keep at it. Well, the sad truth is I never DID get back to Le Mans. The way my career shifted, things just moved in a different direction.

That's the thing about racing – it's a whirlwind. One minute you're on top of the world, the next you're looking for a new ride. Had a pretty nasty crash a couple years later. Pomona Grand Prix. Ripped the suspension clean out of a Maserati. Spent some time in hospital. While I was laid up, started to think. Racing was my whole life, but...was it the ONLY life I wanted?

Met this girl meanwhile, beautiful actress named Joan Freeman. Turns out, she didn't care a lick about my lap times. Loved me for me, which was a new sensation for your boy Bruce, let me tell you. We got hitched, settled down, and that's when Hollywood came knocking.

See, I'd dabbled a bit in movies while I was racing. Knew a few folks in the business. Turns out, being able to handle a high-powered machine at breakneck speeds is a pretty good skill for a stunt driver. Next thing you know, I'm trading racing stripes for greasepaint. Did a bunch of car chase scenes, motorcycle stuff, even a western or two. Got to work with some real legends of the screen. Steve McQueen... now there was a character. Taught me a thing or two about looking cool under pressure!

But the movies, that was a whole different beast. Less about pure skill, more about timing, and faking it 'til you make it. See, with racing, if you screw up, the consequences are real. With movies, worst case scenario you hear the director yell "Cut!" and everyone has a good laugh. Low risk, high reward in some ways.

One time, I was shooting this picture, can't for the life of me remember the title. They had me driving an old jalopy, rigged to blow up on cue. I had to jump out just before the explosion. Well, first take, door gets jammed. Second take, the explosion's a dud. Third take...well let's just say they got the shot, along with me scrambling out with my pants singed a tad!

The director, real old-school type, comes up to me afterwards. "Kessler," he says, stern as anything, "That was the most realistic piece of acting I've ever seen!"

Turns out, that shot made it into the final movie. Guess sometimes, real fear beats any script.

Now, I wouldn't trade those Hollywood years for anything. Met a whole cast of new characters, made some lifelong friends. But the track, it always called me back in some way. Started doing a bit of vintage racing, historic events and the like. That's how I got involved with the Monterey Historics, helped organize those for a good long stretch. Got to see the evolution of the sport, you know? From those classic machines I'd started with, all the way up to the modern beasts.

And wouldn't you know it, there I am at Laguna Seca. Years have gone by, but that track...it's in your blood. See all these young bucks out there, revving their engines, think they're hot stuff. Just like me and Lance back in the day! Well, one thing leads to another, and I end up taking a classic Porsche out for a few demonstration laps. Just for old time's sake, mind you.

Well, maybe I got a bit competitive. May have pushed it a little harder than was strictly "demonstration" pace. Next thing I know, folks are coming up, shaking my hand, telling me I still got it. That felt good, I won't lie. Even better than some of those old victories, if I'm being honest.

See, the thing about racing, it's not about the trophies on the shelf. Well, not just about that. It's the feeling. The freedom when you hit that perfect line through a corner, the rush when you know you're right on the edge. And it's about the people. The guys in the pits, sweating alongside you. The guys you pass on the straightaway, respect in their eyes...or maybe a bit of fear, that was good too! And it's those moments, like at Laguna Seca, when you realize that even though the years go by, that feeling, that connection...that never fades.

Someone asked me once, if I could do it all again, would I? Hell yeah, I would. Maybe take a few less risks, learn to relax a bit more off the track. But the racing itself? The speed, the adrenaline...wouldn't change that for the world. Maybe in the next life, I'll come back as a piston or something, keep the connection going.

Funny thing though, what sticks with me now, it's not the checkered flags or the champagne showers. It's the quiet moments. The time Lance stood up for me in front of Mr. Jones at Lime Rock. The look on Coke Senelle's face as she realized I wasn't exactly falling for her charms. Hawthorn's smile as he held up traffic on Sunset. My wife, Joan, waiting with a warm towel and a cold drink after a long day on the track. It's those moments, the ones in between the noise, that really make a life.

So that's my story, more or less. Probably could ramble on for hours more, truth be told. Lotta miles under these wheels, y'know? But I figure that's enough for now. If anyone out there's got a thirst for more, and a bottle of Hawthorn's favorite scotch handy, well, you know where to find me!

Porsche and the Unblown Engine

Okay, so Le Mans. The big one. 21 years old, fresh-faced American kid, stepping into the European spotlight. I'm teamed up with Ed Hugus, decent guy, but let's just say...he doesn't burn rubber quite like I do. Wasn't too familiar with him then, but, well, he was safe. And with all those eyes on me, the new guy, I had to keep my nose clean. No wild driving, no pushing the Porsche RS past its limits. See, I cut my teeth on Formula 3, where you gotta finesse those cars or you're in the ditch.

First practice, I take it steady. Conservative, even. Thing is, Porsche's number one car that year wasn't a regular RS like mine, it was some fancy prototype. Driven by their hotshot Italian, along with a big-wig German driver. Turns out, that car's a lemon. Steering issues, the works. Meanwhile, yours truly is quietly lapping the track, not breaking any speed records, but consistent. Well, wouldn't you know, by the end of the week, I'm the fastest Porsche.

Now, let's talk about that driver's meeting. Husky Von Hanstein, the Porsche big boss, looks like he stepped right outta some war movie. Asks us all our religions, y'know, 'in case of death' and all that. I say "Jewish", and there's this...pause. Name like 'Kessler', nobody expects that. But things move on, until the next day, when bam! They announce I blew my engine during practice. Blew it! Unheard of for a guy like me. I knew damn well that car was fine when I brought it back to the pits. Tonner, John Bouse, everyone there, they knew it was total bull.

But then, Von Hanstein drops another bombshell. The savior Bruce Kessler, he's gonna bounce from car to car depending on who needs him! Yeah, right. They wanted to replace me with some Dutch driver, some Count-this or Baron-that, all 'cause they could cut a deal with his fancy family. Everyone was riled up – I was riled up! Here's my big break, first Le Mans, and they're treating me like some spare tire.

Well, the race went on, and you might find some pics of me on the podium after. All smiles, getting congratulated... but I never even touched the wheel. Still, all the drama got me noticed. The Brits, bless 'em, got a real kick out of the whole thing – hated those Germans, especially back then. Started calling me 'Lampshade'…real classy, right? But hey, bad publicity is still publicity.

What mattered was, I caught the eye of Centro Sud. Those Italians, always on the lookout for fresh blood. Mimo Dei, he owned the team, saw dollar signs with a bunch of American drivers, a whole marketing angle. Me, I was good with whatever. So, off I go to Modena for a Formula One test with them. Problem is, their cars are relics compared to the new stuff. Still, I manage to match the lap times of Jean Behra, champion of France! More good press, and Mimo starts cooking up plans for "Team America" – me, Gregory, Shelby...talk about a wild crew. I remember those strategy meetings: Mimo speaking a mile a minute in Italian, Masten trying to reply in broken English...priceless.

Point is, that's how the Europeans started to take me seriously. Next thing I knew, I was testing a D-type Jaguar in England. One of those used ones the big teams pass on, y'know? Then Lance, he gets this gleam in his eye. "Let's go check out Lister," he says. We'd heard about this guy Archie Scott Brown – disabled driver, but lightning fast in Bernie Ecclestone's Lister Jag. Imagine that, FIA wouldn't let him race outside England 'cause of his hand, but he was putting Lister on the map.

Naturally, me and Lance start scheming, picturing that car with a Chevy engine instead. Well, we go see Lister. Place is a glorified shed, I swear. Lance is all business, talking to Brian Lister, pointing and gesturing, while I'm at the back just taking it in. Afterwards, Lance comes over, full of fire. "What'd you think?" he asks. I shrug, like, "looks like a car?". That's when Lance snaps. "Bruce, that thing's a piece of junk!" Starts going on about the chassis, the suspension...stuff only an engineer like him could fully appreciate. I'm just nodding along, not wanting to look dumb. But then he says it: "We could build better." Just like that. And that, folks, is how the whole Scarab idea was born.

Building the Scarab

We get back home, and that idea's burning a hole in our heads. Build our own car, outshine Lister, run those Europeans ragged... sounded crazy, even to us. But Lance, he wasn't the type to sit around. Starts hunting down engineers, guys like Chuck Pelly, Phil Remington...top-flight talent. Me, I'm the driver, the test mule, so to speak. But I'm helping too, making runs to the junkyard, picking up whatever we could scavenge.

Now, remember, this is the 50s, not some high-tech racing lab. Our workshop was basically Lance's garage. We were building this monster from the ground up, fueled by guts and maybe a little arrogance. People told us we were nuts, that we'd never beat the Europeans at their own game. Maybe they were right, but we didn't give a damn.

Months go by, and the Scarab starts to take shape. That Chevy engine we dropped in? A beast, roaring to life for the first time...man, you felt that in your bones. The bodywork, all sleek curves – a beauty compared to those boxy Listers. There were setbacks, of course. Things blowing up, parts failing, that's part of the game. But we'd fix it, learn from it, come back stronger. Lance, he was obsessed with making that thing the perfect racing machine.

Finally, it was ready. Time to show the world what we'd cooked up. First few races were rough, let's be honest. Teething problems, learning to work as a team, all of that. But we were fast, damn fast. And we were turning heads. Started getting invitations to big events – Riverside, Laguna Seca...those were our stomping grounds.

Remember those early races against Carroll Shelby in his Maserati? Talk about a rivalry! We'd go wheel-to-wheel, pushing each other to the limit. Shelby was a force to be reckoned with, but we gave him a run for his money every time. And the crowds, they loved it. Underdogs biting at the heels of the establishment.

Then came the big wins. Laguna Seca, beating out the Ferrari boys on their own turf...that was sweet. Still got the trophy on my shelf. We even went back to Europe, showed 'em what an American team could do. People started taking notice – Enzo Ferrari himself, I heard, asked who the hell those guys in that blue car were. That felt pretty damn good, I won't lie.

But racing, man, it's a rollercoaster. For every high, there's a low. We had our share of crashes, mechanical failures, races where it just wasn't our day. There was the time at Nassau, leading the whole damn race, only to have a driveshaft snap on the last lap. Heartbreaking, but you dust yourself off and move on.

The Scarab project, well, it didn't last forever. Racing's expensive, and even with Lance's money, we were always chasing sponsors. Teams come and go, that's the nature of the sport. But those few years, building that car from nothing, racing it...they were some of the best of my life.

Besides the trophies and the busted knuckles, I mean. First, I learned that there's nothing quite like that feeling – pushing a machine to its absolute limits, knowing you're right on the razor's edge. Doesn't matter if you're at Le Mans or some dusty track in the middle of nowhere, that adrenaline rush is universal.

Second, it's about the team. The guys in the pits, sweating alongside you, the engineers who turn your wild ideas into reality, the fans who cheer even when you lose...You can't do it alone. Racing teaches you that, whether you like it or not.

And maybe the biggest lesson is, it's never JUST about winning. Sure, it's sweet. But the battles along the way, the lessons learned, the friendships forged in the fire...those are the things that stick with you long after the checkered flag falls.

The Scarab Years: Memories from the Fast Lane

Bruce Kessler appears quite pleased after trying out the much talked about Lance Reventlow "Mystery Car." The Chevrolet engined Special broke existing track records at California's Willow Springs and at Phoenix, Arizona.

So, Lance looks at me, all serious, and says, "What do you think of what I said?" And I'm like, "Yeah, fine, whatever." Then he gets this glint in his eye. "Bruce, we could build a better car than that Lister." And me, being the brilliant engineer I am, I just nod and say, "Yeah."

That, right there, that's how the whole Scarab thing kicked off. We head back home. Lance and Simone, they had this apartment up near Doheny. We plop down on the floor, and I start rattling off what my dream race car should be – a mix of everything I'd driven. No split axle, good suspension, all that jazz. I'm no expert, mind you, just talking about feel, what worked and what didn't. They're taking notes, making lists...that was the Scarab's birth certificate, right on that apartment floor.

So, Warren moves his shop, brings in new people. Me, I retire from my illustrious day job, 'cause I'm a professional race driver now, don't you know! They hire Ken Miles. Now, Ken, brilliant guy, but he had a whole different vision than my kinda patchwork idea. Problem was, we'd already started down my path, and so that's where the Scarab went. Warren started gathering the crew: Harold Day, Chuck Pelly, Troutman and Barnes, Goons and Travelers... they became the team.

Ken, of course, wasn't down with workin' off someone else's plan. Good ideas, the guy had, but my idea wasn't half-bad either. You take the best of what's out there, build your own Frankenstein monster of a car...that was my way, and we stuck with it.

Now, here's a fun little secret: Goons and Travelers, those guys were Vukovich's mechanics at Indy. Vukey, hell of a driver. Anyway, their boss – name's on the USC hospital, escapes me right now – he did something radical. Usually, owners split the winnings 50/50 with the driver. This guy? He gave half to the driver, half to the whole crew! Made 'em famous as the "rich kids."

They also, wouldn't you know it, got their hands on a Mercedes-Benz 300 SLR. See, Ford had it on loan, and they hired Goons and Travelers to sneak back in every night, strip that engine down, and blueprint it. Mercedes tech, right in Ford's backyard – that kinda thinking went into the Scarab. Well, Ford got the blueprints...and so did Goons and Travelers. A lot of that went into our Formula One car later, but that's another story.

Anyway, Warren's the glue in all this, underappreciated the man was. He knew who to find, how to listen, get the most out of everyone, including yours truly and Lance. If it wasn't for me...okay, I'm kidding. But back in the day, Lance needs a lawyer, I don't know jack about lawyers, but I know this guy Stan Mullen. Sweet old fella, but tough as nails. Becomes Lance's lawyer, keeps everyone on the straight and narrow. I was the matchmaker in the early days, Warren had the brains to keep it running.

Speaking of, we're building the car, out by Jefferson, and guess what? All the astronauts start showing up, wanting to meet us. That's how we ended up in those orange coveralls – copied the spacemen, who now wear what prisoners did back then, funny how that works. Made us stand out for sure.

At one point, Lance says to me, "We gotta get a proper designer on this body." I'm like, sure, whatever. He's the one all fired up, so off I go to the Art Center over on 3rd. You should've seen the looks I got when I pitch up talking about race cars! But then, this one kid in the back, Chuck Pelly, puts his hand up. Just like that, we got our guy. Probably 19, while I'm the grand old man at 21...shows you how things work, huh?

The Scarab's evolving, and I'm the test driver. Thing is, I just described what the car DID, not how to fix it. My job was feeling it out. Meanwhile, I wasn't gonna sit around waiting. Europe calls, I go race, build my own rep. The Scarab was amazing, but it wasn't my whole world, not even then.

Now, one weekend, we're getting ready for a big race, I think it was Riverside. We've got the Scarab all tuned up, but I'm getting restless. Figure, why not enter myself in a different class too? Warren looks at me like I'm crazy, but hey, I'm young and hungry, right? So, I go out, qualify in the Scarab, then hop into this little Porsche Spyder that's sitting around. Smallest engine in the whole damn race. Everyone's laughing, thinking it's a joke.

Well, starts raining like hell. The big guys, they're spinning out left and right, can't handle it. But me, I love the wet. That little Spyder, light as a feather, I'm dancing through the puddles. End up winning my class in the Scarab, and wouldn't you know, almost pulled off a win in the Porsche too. If a hose hadn't blown, I might've had 'em both. After that, they didn't question my sanity so much.

Then there was Chuck Daigh. Brilliant driver, crazy as a loon. He joins the team, and the first thing he does is try and kill us all. We're testing at...think it was Palm Springs? – hot as hell. Chuck, he's always wearing this thick wool sweater. Won't take it off, even on a racetrack. Gets in the car, and before you know it, heat stroke. Passes out at the wheel, Scarab goes careening off into the desert. Luckily no one's hurt, but damn, you gotta keep an eye on that guy!

Chuck though, he recovers, and becomes our go-to driver. Me, I'm off chasing my own thing more and more. There was this one offer...Ferrari, wants me for the Targa Florio. Sicily, crazy road race. Now, they had a reputation for, well, let's just say their safety standards weren't great. But it's FERRARI, right? Well, I get over there, and take one look around. The roads, lined with these stone walls…the spectators, inches from the track...it was madness. I tell them, "No way. I'm not getting in that car."

Now, I get people thought I was chicken. Hell, maybe I was, a little. But see, I wasn't just some hotshot kid anymore. I knew the risks, and I knew when the odds were stacked too high. Walked away from that one, no regrets. See, the thing about racing those days...there was a funeral every other week. Guys I'd raced with, friends...gone. It makes you think. Makes you appreciate when you get to walk away in one piece.

But, like I said, the racing bug bites you hard. While the Scarab was in its prime, Shelby came down to race us. Maseratis, those cars were gorgeous. We went neck and neck, those were some of the best battles I ever had. Turns out, after one race, Shelby finds out his fuel tank's been leaking this whole time. He could've blown up out there! That's the razor's edge for you. Shelby, him and I, we got along well. Became rivals, but there was respect.

We even tried to work together at one point. Late in the Scarab's life, we got this idea – combine American power with European handling. The Scarab-Offy was born. Beautiful car...never quite worked right. See, the Offy engine, it vibrated like crazy.

Shook the whole damn chassis apart. Still, we tried, we went for it, and that's what mattered.

The whole Scarab project...it didn't last forever. Money gets tight, that's always the way with racing. But even now, people come up to me, tell me about seeing those blue cars out on the track. Tell me we inspired them, that we proved Americans could build our own machines and take on the world. That, honestly, that means more than any checkered flag.

You know, those were wild times, back in the early days of the Scarab. We were young, fueled by this crazy belief that we could do the impossible. And in a way, we did. But racing back then, it was different. The cars were less forgiving, the tracks more dangerous. There was a real sense of camaraderie, and also a sense of...well, that anything could happen.

I think about guys like Masten Gregory. Brilliant driver, crazy sense of humor. Him and I, we did an endurance race together. Now, the rule was you had to stop for fuel at a certain point. Well, Masten, he's always pushing the limits. We're almost out of gas, and he still won't pit. I'm yelling at him, everyone's screaming...finally, the car sputters to a stop, right on the damn track. Masten, he just gets out, cool as you please, and starts hitchhiking! Got a tow back to the pits, still smiling. That was Masten.

Bruce Kessler (3) and Joakim Bonnierare left sitting on the grid when their engines failed to start during Saturday's practice.

Then there were the fans. You wouldn't believe some of the places we raced. Dusty little tracks in the middle of nowhere, crowds packed in, cheering us on. We'd sign autographs for kids on our greasy overalls, pose for pictures next to the cars...it felt like we were part of something bigger, even when we were just a ragtag team with a homemade car.

Of course, there were the fancy events too. Nassau Speed Week, that was a whole scene. Celebrities, high rollers...and there we were, California kids, mixing it up with European royalty. We even had some wild parties at Lance's house. I remember one where someone – I'm not naming names – decided to use Lance's priceless antique armor as a coat rack. Lance wasn't too pleased about that, let me tell you.

But through it all, the best times were in the pits. The crew, those guys were family. Working late nights, sweating together, arguing, laughing...there's a bond that forms when you're all fighting for the same thing, even if that thing is just getting a temperamental car to the start line.

The Scarab years faded out. Things change, teams move on. But those memories... they stay with you. The smell of race fuel, the roar of the crowd, the feeling of the wheel in your hands as you push a car to its absolute limit...those never really go away.

And you know what else? I learned something about myself in that time. I learned that I wasn't just a racer. I was an entrepreneur too, a team player, a leader sometimes. The Scarab project, it forced me to grow up fast, to be more than just the guy behind the wheel. And those lessons, well, they served me well in everything I did afterwards.

Racing, it's in your blood, sure. But it's also in your head, and in your heart. It teaches you to take risks, to embrace those moments where everything's on the line, and to keep going even when the odds are against you. And those lessons, well, they apply whether you're on the racetrack or in the boardroom.

SPORTS CARS ILLUSTRATED
50¢ MARCH 1960
design · economy · competition
DODGE AND DAIMLER V8'S ROAD-TESTED
BIG FORMULA JUNIOR ROUNDUP
SEBRING WINNER BRUCE MCLAREN
SCARAB AND CLIMAX CUTAWAYS

I Wasn't Loyal to One Car, But Damn Was I Fast

Chuck shows up at the shop on Jefferson, and it's time to start slapping a body onto this beast. Now, a race car at the end of the day...it's just a chassis, an engine, a whole pile of parts. Chuck took one look and started figuring out the shape, but there's only so wild you can get at that time, y'know?

We build the first body, I take it out for testing. Of course, I end up running it off the road, denting the front a tad. Hey, it's all tin, right? Anyway, gives us a chance to rethink things. Chuck decides to go narrower up front, start fine-tuning. We figured, why make the thing bigger than it had to be?

Now, the first real race where anybody ever saw the Scarab...we did most of our testing at Willow Springs back then. I gotta think...was Riverside even built yet? Few places to properly run a car like that. Anyway, it was February of '58...no, hold up, I got that wrong. 'Cause I had just come off the Grand Prix of Cuba. Lance says the Scarab's debut race is Phoenix, SCCA event. And his main rival? Dan Gurney in Frank Arciero's Ferrari. Hell of a combo, that.

We fly the team out in Lance's Cessna 310, and then get the bombshell: they won't let Lance race! I mean, this is after the announcements, the whole build-up. Lance is of age, totally legal, got the skills...and they pull this crap. Lance, cool as ever, says "Bruce, you drive."

Me? I go to Warren, say "Look, I don't want to steal Lance's thunder. First race, it's his car." We try and reason with the officials. No dice. Now, here's the thing: they say I can drive, because of my birthday being a month after Lance's. So, okay, I get it. First time anyone outside the team's ever laid eyes on the Scarab, and it has no paint job even!

Practice starts. Car's got this fuel issue in hard right turns. Keeps starving, the engine cuts out for a second, then kicks back in. Still, we're turning fast laps. Then comes the moment...I'm out there, and who do I see but Gurney. He's taking this big, fast bend, all those little steering corrections you do at 120 miles an hour. I'm watching over his shoulder, and I just...I go past. I WHOOSH right by him! And right then it hits me: this car…it's THE answer. This is what we've been working towards.

That's what I remember from those first tests. We got Richard Ginther in the car later, fixed the fuel thing. He comes out, says the same damn thing. Lance wanted me to race the thing, but I said no. That was his baby.

See, I was never the type to be loyal to just one team. If someone had a good car, I wanted a shot behind the wheel. Loved the Scarab crew, but a racer's gotta race. That first outing, the bare metal, that narrow front end...that was how the world saw it for the first time. Later, we got it to look prettier, sure.

Now, about that fuel injection...American cars still didn't have that. We got ours from a guy, damn, his name escapes me, but he made 'em for Indy cars. Problem was, those tubes were all wrong for a gas engine. Chuck was working on the hood with all that in mind, and honestly, back then? We had a 50/50 chance of starting the car and it bursting into flames. Put it out, then keep the engine running, that was the drill! Hood down, and off you go.

We'd actually start 'em with the hood still up. Everything was experimental when the Scarab project first started. But here's the thing, and nobody talks about this: all the stuff going on behind the scenes, the little stories that didn't make the magazines...that's the history that still needs telling.

So, I'm back east, racing for North American Ferrari with Phil Hill and Gurney. Big names. Meanwhile, the Scarab boys are killing it out West. Come October, it's the Times Grand Prix – huge deal. First time we're running three cars in a race, bringing in those European drivers, which means the race is longer, and guess what? We don't have enough fuel in our tanks for that.

Now, here's the plan (or, well, the story, depending on who you ask). We tell everyone all three cars are good to go the distance. That's a lie. They left my car alone, knowing it'd run out. The idea was, I'd lead, burn up Phil Hill, then clear the way for Lance and Chuck. Sneaky strategy, right?

The other thing Lance was trying...see, he counted up all the right-hand turns versus the left on the track. Figured, if we set his car up to favor the rights, he'd make up time. Good in theory, not so much in practice. But hey, we're giving it a shot. Just don't tell anyone, okay?

So the plan is set – I'm the pacesetter, gonna draw Phil into a duel he can't win, then step aside. I'm cool with it. Lance with his wedged-up car, Chuck with a normal setup... should be interesting.

Race weekend arrives. Blazing hot. Gotta qualify. Chuck? Sticks it on pole! Now, me, I'm playing it slow. Don't want to tip our hand, just need that break at the start to make this scheme work.

Lance shows up, all set with this car designed to only turn one way. Second day of practice, he goes off on some measly left-hander, bends the chassis good. Car's toast, and the race hasn't even begun. So much for that theory.

Now, this is where I maybe don't think things through. Dan Hill and I are neck and neck for the overall championship. This race counts, and Lance comes up with a bright idea: wants to co-drive my car. I say sure, whatever. Then he says, "Can I start?" I figure, okay...and that, friends, was my downfall. Guy's different from me under pressure, let's just say that.

Race starts, and he either stalls it or blows the launch. Von Trips in the Ferrari tags our back end. Officials black flag him – safety check! – which means pits, first lap. Chaos. Next lap, Lance comes in, the back comes off, no leaks... they clear him to go. He looks at me, says, "You drive."

Helmet? Who knows where the thing is! I scramble, grab it, jump in. Problem is, our pits are on the far end. By the time I get out there, I'm full-tilt, over 100 miles an hour, headed for turn one, looking for a gap to get back into the race. Just then, red flag.

"Holy crap," I think, slamming the brakes. I look back, see Lance, Warren, the whole crew charging down pit lane. They get to the officials' stand, it's arguing, yelling...then suddenly, Lance throws a punch! Straight up decks some official! Newspapers went wild over it. He was *that* mad.

So, there I am, sitting in the car, no clue what's going on. No word from the flagman, nothing. I'm watching the officials' stand...they're having some heated discussions, but what the hell was happening? Lance slugging someone over fuel tanks? Come on!

The story goes that they'd disqualified us – all three cars. Lance, he wasn't having any of that. Stormed over to argue, things got physical, and bam! International incident right there on the track.

Turns out, the race got stopped, but only for like a minute. I missed the restart completely, sitting there like an idiot! Even then, we weren't technically out. The disqualification only hits once the race is done, y'know, paperwork stuff.

Now, here's where it gets real interesting. I make the turn, head back towards the pits...and the race is still going! Cars whizzing by like I'm parked. Talk about confusing!

They tell me to get in the pits, stat. Whole crew's waiting, and here's the bombshell: they want me to get back in the car and finish the damn race. Problem is, I'm not the only one with that idea.

See, Augie Pabst was driving Chuck Daigh's car at this point. He'd brought it in thinking it needed fuel...turns out, it didn't! They fill the tank anyway, figuring why not? But here's the catch – the pit rules were different back then. You couldn't refuel a car until the driver had been out for a set amount of time. Augie's just sitting there, waiting, and now they want him to take over from me? Messy with a capital M.

In the end, they settle on a compromise. I stay in, do another 30 laps or so. This is after racing flat-out earlier, mind you. Once the time's up, THEN Augie takes over. Talk about your seat-of-the-pants racing!

We finally finish the thing, hours later than expected, somewhere way back in the pack. And the cherry on top? I won the race. On paper, anyway. Got those points.

See, here's the thing: while the big drama was happening with Lance, the officials completely lost track of who was in which car. When they finally figured it out, turns out I'd done the most laps while in the lead. Technically, winner. Not exactly the way I'd planned on it, but hey, I'll take it.

But you know what else? That race cost me the championship. Dan Hill ended up ahead. And it was all because, at that crucial moment, I said "sure" instead of thinking it through. Lesson learned the hard way, that's for damn sure.

Looking back, though, those were crazy times. Rules were more like guidelines, and nobody was afraid to bend 'em, or break 'em outright if they thought they could get away with it. You had to be on your toes, ready for anything. Kind of racing you don't see anymore, for better or worse.

So, they red flag me for some reason, I'm sitting there clueless. Then, here's the starting line, we're one-two-three on the grid, and BAM, everything changes. Chuck being Chuck, decides to mess with the gear ratios. Halibrand rear ends, the quick-change kind. Dude was a genius, both behind the wheel and with the wrench. Figures out some secret advantage or whatever, and here we are on the grid, taking the bloody rear end apart!

Engines are revving – this ain't the time or place for that kind of work! They slap it back together just as the flag's about to drop. If you ask me, we were lucky to even finish the race after that stunt.

Anyway, Chuck ends up winning, wouldn't you know it. And Phil Hill? His car gives up the ghost. The heat fried the thing. That race...was a dogfight the whole damn way until Phil just couldn't keep up. Classic stuff, and makes for a great story.

But lemme tell you, the REAL story, the stuff nobody ever talks about, that's where it gets wild. That whole race was planned out – not the gear ratio bit, that was vintage Chuck – but the rest...well, it wasn't exactly above board. And then on top of that, we got Nassau coming up right after. They take Chuck and Lance's cars, and I end up getting recruited by Ferrari.

#3 Bruce Kessler, #82 Wayne Wheeler, Ken Miles   Pomona March '59

Imagine that! Driving the 4.9, the one Shelby won so much with, for John Edgar. 'Course, getting to Nassau was its own adventure, but that's a tale for another time.

Now, here's something else from around then...Lance. Guy had gotten into his head that I wasn't right after Le Mans. The accident, the guy getting killed in that car...nothing to do with me, but Lance was convinced I had some kinda mental thing going on. Even runs the USAC races by me as proof. Says I'm driving a car I hate, still finishing in the money, that means there's something wrong with me. Next thing I know, he's talking to my mother!

Tells her I need therapy, all because of the Le Mans crash. And since he's Lance, he lines up the "top psychiatrist in Beverly Hills" for me. Figured, what the hell, might as well. Worst case scenario, I get a few hours off from dealing with Lance's theories.

So, I go see this shrink, and he launches into the whole "tell me about your childhood" routine. I cut him off. "Look," I say, "Lance sent me, thinks I'm about to off myself. Got a problem with that, let's talk about it."

Well, that did not go down like the doc expected. He starts stammering, trying to backtrack, gets all flustered. I just stare at him, waiting. Finally, he admits Lance is the one who's worried, not him. Can you believe that?

So, I tell him flat out, "I'm fine. Lance is full of it, like always. This whole thing is a waste of time." Walk out and leave him sitting there. Report back to Lance, too. Tell him, "Your shrink agrees with me, not you." He didn't like that one bit, let me tell you.

The thing is, Lance was always in his own head. Brilliant guy, but could overthink things, get all wound up. That's why he got so fixated on my driving post-Le Mans. Couldn't see that I was back on track, doing well for myself.

Anyway, Nassau. We get down there, and wouldn't you know it, Ferrari's there with their new Dino 246s. Sleek little things, but with those V6 engines, they just didn't have the grunt of the Scarabs. Weather, though…that was brutal. Humid as hell, rain on and off, turns the track into this greasy mess.

We go out for practice, and I'm flying. Figure, why not push it, see what the car can do? Rain's coming down sideways, and suddenly I realize...brakes are gone. Pedal hits the floor, nothing! Straight into the hay bales at the end of the straight I go. Luckily, those things slow you down pretty quick, otherwise I'd have been swimming.

Turns out, the heat and humidity cooked my brake fluid. Boiled it right in the lines. Not the most confidence-boosting start to a big race, I'll tell you that. Got the fluid swapped out, but man, that feeling of the pedal going dead while you're hauling ass...that stays with you.

Race day itself was a whole different beast. Sun came out, dried the track, turned it all slick again. Start is mayhem, as usual. Now, the Dinos had better handling on the tight corners, but on the straights, the Scarabs had 'em beat for pure speed.

Chuck and Lance get out front, and what follows is one of the best races I've ever seen, even though I wasn't the one driving. They're swapping the lead, pushing each other, the Ferraris trying to outsmart 'em...great spectacle.

Then, halfway through, here comes the rain again. Track turns into a slip-and-slide. The Ferraris, they start dropping like flies. Those little V6s, they just don't like the wet. But the Scarab, big Chevy V8 with all that torque...that thing just powered through.

Chuck ends up taking the win, Lance right behind him. One-two finish for the homebuilt cars. You should've seen the faces of the Ferrari guys! That, right there, is what the Scarab project was all about...showing those European teams that Americans could do it just as well, if not better.

That night, we partied. Hell, we partied most nights down there, if I'm being honest. Nassau in those days, it was wild. But that win, it felt special. Vindication, after all the work, all the doubters. Those are the moments you race for.

Now, here's the thing about those Nassau victories... They didn't exactly heal the rift between me and Lance. He was still convinced I wasn't "all there" driving-wise. It was frustrating, being doubted like that, especially from someone I considered a friend. Made me even more determined to prove him wrong.

That led me to do some riskier things, maybe. Looking back, I was young, hungry, and maybe a touch reckless. Part of being a race car driver is pushing limits, but sometimes you push them too far. The next year at Nassau, that's exactly what happened.

We take a new Scarab down, the Mk II. Lighter, faster, but less stable than the old ones. It's also got experimental disc brakes. They're powerful, but prone to overheating. Sure enough, same as the year before, we get practice runs in the wet. Brakes are fine. Then race day comes, and the sun is blazing.

I make a good start, running near the front of the pack. But every time I brake hard, the pedal starts going down further and further. Those discs are cooking themselves! I try to nurse it, but there's only so much you can do at those speeds. Coming into a tight corner, I lose it. Spin, go off into a ditch.

The car's totaled, I'm lucky to walk away. Lance, of course, sees this as confirmation. Tells me straight up, "See, I told you there was something wrong." That hurt, I won't lie. The thing is, those brakes...that was an engineering issue, not my driving. But try explaining that to Lance when he's got his mind made up.

That crash marked a turning point, not just with Nassau, but with the Scarab team itself. Lance was getting more and more controlling. Warren was loyal, Chuck was focused on the mechanical side, and me...well, I was the loose cannon. Didn't fit into his vision of how things should run, especially after that accident.

We still raced together, still had some good moments. But that sense of teamwork, of being a family like in the early days, that was gone. We were all pulling in different directions. Wasn't long before I started looking for opportunities elsewhere. I needed a team where I could be ME, not try to fit some mold Lance had in his head.

Don't get me wrong, I've got nothing but respect for the man. We built something amazing with the Scarab, changed racing history. But we were also like oil and water – great in the right combination, but explosive if you mixed us too closely. Sometimes, even when you win, things still gotta change.

Shrinks

See, the thing about shrinks back then, it was all about digging into your past, mommy issues, daddy issues, the whole Freudian nine yards. So, here I am in this fancy office, the smell of old books and stale coffee hangin' heavy in the air. The guy starts in with the usual "tell me about your childhood" routine, and I put the brakes on that real quick.

"Doc," I say, leanin' back like I own the place, "let's not waste either of our time. Lance Reventlow thinks I'm a loose nut behind the wheel – says I ain't got that killer instinct, that I get too...what's the word? Emotional." The doc just kinda blinks at me for a beat, like he ain't used to someone talkin' straight, then he does the craziest thing a shrink's ever done. He leans back, steeples his fingers, and says:

"Kid, get out of my office. There ain't nothin' wrong with you."

Now, I ain't one to question the experts, so I do just that. Next thing you know, it's Nassau – and if you think Vegas is wild, you ain't seen nothin' yet. That whole island turns into a circus come race week, all palm trees and paradise by day, and pure, unadulterated chaos by night.

I'm behind the wheel of the big '49 Ferrari, Shelby's in the '57, and we're both pushin' hard out on the track. And then along comes this guy, Jim Rathman, in...well, it deserves more of a cackle than a description. Some kinda Frankenstein car, half-Maserati, half-Chevy, and the rest held together by spit and baling wire.

I get a little too hot coming into that final corner, nothin' serious, just enough to graze the line of pine trees they'd planted there. Barely a scratch on the paint, but Lance, back in the pits, is goin' absolutely bonkers. "Now that's what I'm talkin' about!" he's yellin', like this is the first time I've actually tried to win a damn race.

Race day comes, and I end up takin' the trophy, shoulda been a night to remember. Instead, it's the start of the craziest 24 hours of my life, all thanks to John Edgar. Now, John, God rest his soul, he liked his liquor...maybe a little too much. Scrawny fella, barely looked like he could hold a glass, but he had this doctor trailin' him – more of a drinkin' buddy than any real medic.

So these big races, you gotta pit – tires, fuel, the whole deal. I'm running on fumes, and Joe Landacre – bless his soul, Mechanic of the Year, mind you! – is waving me in like his arms are on fire. Only problem is, I keep glancing up to that box above our pit. John's up there, swayin' like a palm tree in a hurricane, and just one stiff breeze, well... There ain't gonna be enough left of him to sweep up.

I don't even think, just slam the Ferrari into the pits. The shot of me practically leapin' outta that car ended up on the cover of Sports Car Graphic, I might add. I charge up the stairs, scattering those high-society types sippin' their champagne. I grab John, yank him back from the ledge, yellin' somethin' about not being a bird ready to take flight.

Turns out, the folks in charge had seen the whole thing unfoldin' too, and they weren't taking chances. There's John, skinny as a fencepost, tied to the railin' with his own belt! Well, that takes some of the pressure off, but now my blood's pumpin' double-time. I race back downstairs...and that's when the other shoe drops. The gear lever snaps clean off in my hand. Seems Joe-freakin'-Landacre, instead of orderin' a replacement, just welded the cracked one back together. Championship on the line, and I'm sittin' in a glorified go-kart.

But that's racin' for ya. Ain't no time to dwell – Chuck Daigh's car craps out, Lance sees opportunity like a hawk eyein' a mouse, and bellows at Chuck to take the wheel mid-way through his pit stop. Chuck, cool as you like, doesn't even hesitate. He's still fumblin' with his helmet as he slides into the car and tears off like the devil's after him. And damn if he doesn't win the whole thing!

Meanwhile, whichever Rodriguez brother it was – swear those two were like whirlwinds – is supposed to be on a plane to New York. Big publicity stunt, get him on TV or some such nonsense. Of course, his flight's delayed. The whole victory banquet – black tie affair, the whole shebang – is on hold.

1Bruce with Bill Sadler

John Edgar, well, he starts takin' the news like a cat bein' tossed in a bathtub. His words get sloppier, the drinks keep comin', and pretty soon he lets out an F-bomb that has half the room blushin' and the other half grinnin'. Rodriguez finally shows up, lookin' a little worse for wear, and, well, that night gets messy. Real messy.

The madness ain't over, not by a long shot. Those bigwigs are kickin' off this nonstop jet service to New York, packed with drivers, team owners, you name it – another dog-and-pony show for the press. And there's the owner of the Sadler, nice enough fella, sharp suits, distributor for KLG spark plugs. That Sadler, now, it was somethin' else. Fast as hell...until it went kaput, that is. But lemme tell ya, there's nothin' quite like takin' off in one of those early jets. Felt like we were strapped to a rocket.

Bill Sadler...what a character. As old as my grandaddy, bless his soul, with the kindest smile you ever did see. That Sadler of his, now that was a different beast altogether – fast as hell when it behaved, but prone to more fits than a stable of unbroken horses. Still, after seeing her run, it got the gears turning in my head. Ferrari didn't have nothin' lined up for the Examiner Grand Prix, Phil Hill wasn't running, neither was Dan Gurney ... no big names, really, and I was starting to get restless.

The thing about the Examiner was, they were desperate for drivers with some recognition. Even pulling in guys from Europe to fill out their roster. So I figure, why not throw my hat in the ring? I tell 'em, half-joking, that I'll drive a Scarab, even though Lance Reventlow had those beauties locked up tight since it was the start of the '59 season. Then, just for the heck of it, I toss in that I might be interested in taking a Sadler to the track if there happened to be a spare.

Now, I wasn't expecting much. But wouldn't you know it, Bill calls my bluff! Turns out, they'd built a second Sadler and it was mine for the taking, if I wanted it. This, my friends, is how I stumbled into my last real race, and what a wild ride it turned out to be!

Lance – God rest his soul, stubborn as a mule that man was – grudgingly agrees to be my pit chief. Phil Remington and Harold Day, they promise to handle the mechanics. It was a bit of a reunion, a bittersweet one, knowing this would likely be our last hurrah together. And there was Bill Sadler, beamin' from ear to ear like a proud father, even with his car causin' us headaches from the get-go.

See, those Sadlers, they were beautifully built, but temperamental wasn't the half of it. Qualifying rolls around, and I'm chugging along, thinkin' I've got a decent lap goin'...when she just sputters and dies. Not a gradual loss of power, mind you, it was like someone flipped a switch. Get towed back to the pit, swearin' up and down somethin' must have busted, but we can't find the problem for the life of us.

Bill, he keeps insistin', "I know what it is, I know what it is," with this glint in his eye that makes me a bit suspicious. In the end, it takes Phil and Harold, bless their greasy souls, to figure it out. Turns out, all the welding they'd been doin' around the carburetors had somehow clogged one of 'em with gunk. Explains why it'd run for a spell, then just choke out like you'd cut off its air supply.

Now, Aggie Janian, the promoter – that name brings back memories. Let's just say he was the type who always had an angle. The man sees the whole fiasco with the Sadler, and you know what he does? Offers me a spot in the consolation race. Says if I win, even as an invited driver, he'll let me into the main event, albeit starting dead last. Seemed a long shot, but hey, I've always been up for a challenge.

Lining up for that consolation race, I gotta chuckle. We're talkin' a hodgepodge of cars, some that have no business on a real track. I take off, and halfway to the first corner, it's clear there ain't a single car out there that can keep up with the Sadler. So, I ease off, just cruise on through to take the checkered flag. Come 'round for my victory lap, I tell 'em nope, this car ain't movin' another inch. Let the crew take it back, I've had enough excitement for one day.

Next morning, bright and early, they're all over me, askin' if I'm brakin' hard or puttin' her through any rough stuff. I tell 'em of course I am, it's not exactly a casual drive we're talkin' about. Then they drop the bombshell – turns out, they had the Sadler on the rack last night and had to weld the chassis in, what was it, seven places? My mind's racin', trying to remember if I'd hit any bad bumps, but they swear up and down she'll hold together, no worries there.

So there I am, lined up for the big race, dead last in a pack of 33. Al Torres – heck of a starter, that guy – does his usual checks, makin' sure we're strapped in. He gets to me, I've got my belt all ready...then the moment he turns to start the race, I drop it. See, us drivers, we got a rhythm with those starters. Know exactly when he's gonna turn, when he'll hit the flag...and when we're outta there before anyone else can blink. The look on Torres' face when I went tearin' by was priceless.

I pick my way through the pack, and the stories people told of what it looked like...well, let's just say I made an impression. By lap 7, I've gone from 33rd to somewhere near the front, passing cars like they were standing still. People must have thought I'd gone mad, but with that Sadler under me, I felt like I could take on the world.

Comin' up on the straightaway, I see Lance with the pit board, waitin' for the right moment. Then, outta the corner of my eye, I see Chuck Daigh in Murphy's Buick Curtis – now there's a sight you don't see every day – pass the start-finish line. A little wiggle in his tail tells me he's changed gears, something ain't quite right with that Buick. I'm half a straightaway behind, lookin' for my own signal, heart pounding like a drum solo.

That's when I see Old Yellow up ahead. I knew that corner, knew every bump and dip in it. Last thing I remember clear as day is Lance, bless him, holdin' that pit board high. And the message, clear as could be, was "Call your mother."

Then everything just kinda...went blurry. I woke up in the hospital, head fuzzy as cotton, surrounded by the whole crew. Turns out, right at Old Yellow, somethin' snapped. Could have been the chassis, or an axle...no one ever figured it out for sure. Car went flippin' end over end, and it's a miracle I walked away with nothin' worse than a few bruises and a mighty headache.

Doc said I should retire after that. Said the next time I might not be so lucky. Maybe he was right, but part of me wishes I'd taken one more spin around the track. Still, it was a hell of a way to go out, wouldn't you say?

So, what was that all about with Lance and the "Call your mother" sign? Beats me. I just remember staring at him, right there by the start-finish line, and that was the last clear image in my head. The next thing I know, I'm shifting...and there's oil. Too much oil.

Max Balchowsky had blown his engine, the track's slick as ice, and then it happens – I go right into the back of a Royal Park car. The force throws me clean out, and wouldn't you know it, I smack into this poor kid, what, 18 years old? Just standing there, minding his own business. Hit him so hard I broke his arm. I mean, thank God he was there to break my fall, otherwise...well, let's not dwell on that.

Of course, I've got a concussion, the mother of all concussions. Out cold for four days. Apparently, I was talking, but they say I wasn't really "there" you know? The race gets stopped, the whole shebang. Meanwhile, my baby brother Stevie – the poet, that one – and my mom, bless her heart, they'd come to watch. And Mom, she sees it all, sees me go flying, the whole mess, and when I finally wake up...she's fuming. Stevie tells me she stood right up and yelled, "Damn it, I thought Bruce was going to win that one!"

So, I'm in this hospital in Pomona, two big ol' male nurses holding me down 'cause apparently, I was a handful even knocked out. Finally, I come to, head swimming, and first thing I ask is, "What time is it?". They tell me it's 10 in the morning. "Good," I mumble, "I can get back to the track". See, I figured someone had clipped me with a tire, knocked me silly for a bit, thought I could get back in the race. They say, "Uh, it's Thursday."

That's when it starts coming back in blurry pieces. I gotta rebuild my memory, bit by bit. And hey, there's always those weird side stories, right? Before that race, this guy keeps pestering me at the Peterson dinners. "Got somethin' for ya, Bruce. Somethin' I been carrying around..." Turns out, he was chief mechanic for Lubin back in the day!

So, I finally meet the guy for lunch, he spins this whole tale about being the head mechanic for the city of Los Angeles, big important fella now. We head out to his car, he says, "Time to give you this thing I've held onto for 40 years..." And out of his trunk he pulls this...sock. Inside? A regular Cal Club trophy. First in class, 500 cc.

Now, I don't recall running that race. Not a flicker of memory. But the story goes, they got this brand new Norton Cooper, right before the race. Lubin sends this guy to ask if I'd drive it, I say "Sure, why not?", and I go on to win the darn thing. Got the trophy to prove it, sitting right there in my house. But in my head? It's a big blank.

I'm fresh outta the hospital after that Pomona mess. And these F1 guys – the bigwigs who run Formula One, all those fancy pants races – tell me I'm on the bench. Concussion did a number on me, so I'm banned from their tracks for a whole year. Now, I could drive at smaller events, local stuff, but those don't rev my engine, you know? The big leagues, the FI races, that's the only game in town for me. Well, I figure, if that's how it is, then I'm done racin'. Period.

So, they ship me home, and that's when my next-door neighbor – well, a block away – gets involved. Julie Payne, younger than me by a good stretch, but real close with my family. See, she was John Payne, the Western movie star's daughter, and our families go way back. My folks, bless their souls, had that kinda house where anyone was welcome. You could be in a tuxedo, in a swimsuit, didn't matter one bit. Mom and Dad would treat you like family.

Anyways, Julie, she tells her stepfather – Charlie Leder, real bigshot writer at MGM, top of the heap – that I'm outta commission after the crash. Well, wouldn't you know it, Charlie's got a line into this pilot MGM ABC is cooking up. All about sports car racin' of all things! Stars David Jansen, and this other kid, John Ashley, who later became a producer, did a bunch of shows with him.

Charlie puts in a word, and before I know it they want me as a technical advisor! I say, "Sure, why not?" They flash some numbers, not much, but it's a foot in the door, right? So I head over to this fancy lawyer's office – Bautzer, that was his name, handled accounts for Howard Hughes and MGM, the whole nine yards. Bunch of suits, producers, Charlie, the whole lot. Talk about my role, how much I'd make...let's just say it wasn't enough to buy a Ferrari.

Now, here's the kicker – the director on this whole deal is Ted Post. Helluva guy, limped a bit, not sure what that was about. Top-notch director – did one of the Planet of the Apes movies, some big stuff – and a real straight shooter, salt of the earth despite bein' a New Yorker.

So, I'm in Ted's office, and they keep shovin' these scripts my way. "Tell us what's wrong," they say, meanin' the technical bits. Well, I do. I tear those scripts to shreds. "No one talks like this," I tell 'em, "No racer does the stuff you got written here!" Figure it's my job, right? Thing is, each time, those suits get more and more pissed. Rewrite after rewrite, and I keep doin' the same thing.

Finally, another script lands on my lap. I go through my usual spiel, and Ted, he just stares at it, then looks up at me. Doesn't ask about the gear shifts or the pit strategies – he asks, "What'd you think of the story, Bruce?" So I tell him straight: "Ted, with all due respect, I ain't never met a soul who acts like these characters. Don't suppose one of 'em is meant to be me, do ya?" He just grunts, says "What a piece of shit," and hurls the script onto his desk. Then he starts limping around the room, going on about how awful it is.

Buzzer goes off, and it's some head honcho from ABC, all smiles and talkin' up this new draft. Ted lays it on thick, says he's real excited, just a few tweaks and they're golden. Then, as soon as Mr. Big Shot is gone, Ted looks at me and says, "Bruce, what'd you think?" .

Well, I get up, mimic Ted's limp as best I can, and start circling that script. "This," I say, "is a piece of shit!" Ted bursts out laughin', knows I'm playin' him. Then he gets serious. "Look, Bruce," he says, "This John Ashley character, he's kinda sorta based on you. Why don't you go home, write me up a couple of paragraphs – like a mini story pitch, seein' as you know how this world works. I like it, I'll buy it."

So that night, I sit down and I bang out three stories. Treatments, they call 'em. And goddamn if they didn't buy the whole lot! That, folks, was the start, the beginning of the end of my racin' career and the whole Hollywood thing. Trips to New York, meetin' producers...well, that's a whole saga in itself.

One little story about that time...the guard at the MGM gate, Kenneth Hollywood was his name. Sweet guy, bit on the heavy side. First day I report for work, I'm drivin' a

Volkswagen, nothin' fancy. Pull up, give Kenneth my name, and bless him, he tells me where to park, where to find the office, "Thank you, Ken," the whole works.

Fast forward a few years, and I'm rollin' up in a Lamborghini. Belonged to this buddy of mine, Fuad Said, real character. Stop at the gate, and Kenneth, same as always: "Hi Bruce, nice to see you! Stage eight today, your usual parking spot." That's how he was, treated me the same, Volkswagen or Lamborghini, didn't make a damn bit of difference to him. Now that's a real Hollywood guy, and his name was Hollywood, no less!

Oh, and that Lamborghini...man, that thing was a pain in the ass. Crew always had to push-start the damn thing, somethin' wonky with the electrics that no one could fix. A producer on the show wanted to buy it from Fuad, and I did my best to warn him off. That car, I told him, would be nothin' but trouble. Shoulda listened to ol' Bruce, huh?

From Pomona to the World Stage

Alright, let's rewind. Before England, before those big-name European circuits, I was a hotshot kid racing back in California. Pomona, Riverside, all those tracks... that's where I made my bones. I grew up itching for speed, building my own cars, running 'em hard at the local spots. Wasn't about winning trophies; it was that feeling, you know? That surge of power and the rumble under your feet… pure adrenaline. Soon enough, I was mixing it up in sports car races, and that's when things started getting serious.

Now, here's the thing about racing back then, especially for a young buck like me. There wasn't the same kind of safety net. No fancy fireproof suits, no crumple zones in the cars…you were out there, raw, exposed. One wrong move, and it was lights out. But that's part of what fueled the excitement, that danger lurking just around the corner. Made you focus, made you push the limits.

By the time I'm 19, I'm feeling pretty cocky. I've tasted some success, won the 500cc Club of America championship. But I'm hungry for the real deal, those legendary Formula One races in Europe. So, I save up some cash, pack my bags, and I'm on a ship headed for England. No sponsors, no team lined up. I figured I'd show up, hustle my way into a seat, and let my driving do the talking. Looking back, maybe a bit naive, but hell, I was young and fearless.

First few months, I'm sleeping in my car, scraping by on whatever odd jobs I can find. But I'm also getting myself to the tracks, watching, learning, soaking in everything about the European racing scene. It was a whole different animal to what I was used to back home. The cars were faster, the competition fiercer, and the tracks... they were something else. Narrow, winding, unforgiving. Places like Silverstone and Brands Hatch, steeped in history, where the echoes of past champions seemed to hang in the air.

Eventually, I land a gig with a smaller team. Nothing glamorous, but finally, I'm getting behind the wheel of a proper Formula 2 car. And that's where the real education begins. These guys, they don't sugarcoat it. You either perform or you're out on your ear. My first time out, I think I'm flying. Come back in, they tell me I qualified 15th out of 25. 15th! I couldn't wrap my head around it.

That's when the other drivers, guys like Stuart Lewis-Evans and Roy Salvadori – absolute legends – they took me under their wing. Turns out, I was driving like I was scared of breaking the rental car. Every corner, I'm two gears too low, braking too early. "Bruce," they tell me, "You've got to believe in the machine. It's designed to handle way more than you think."

I'll tell you, that advice changed everything. Next practice session, I went out with a different attitude. I squeezed the throttle, tested the limits of grip. I found that fine line between control and chaos, where the car dances under you, and you're one with the track. It was exhilarating and terrifying all at once. And guess what? I jumped near the top of the timesheets.

From then on, it was a rollercoaster ride. One race I'm up there with the big names – Jimmy Clark, Graham Hill – the next I'm fighting just to qualify. Ferrari even came knocking, not for a race seat, mind you, but to test their cars, do the grunt work. It was a humbling honor. See, in those days, testing could be as dangerous as the race itself. You were the guinea pig, pushing those experimental cars until something broke – hopefully, not while you were at the wheel.

Then there's Monte Carlo. Everyone talks about the glamour, but for me, it was pure white-knuckle terror. Those streets, no wider than a goat path, with walls hungry to snatch you up… it was a different kind of racing altogether. I did alright in the car, but watching from the pits? No thanks. I'd seen guys disappear into those corners, and the silence until you know if they're okay… that's a sound that haunts you.

But you know what? That's the thing about racing. It tests you, breaks you down, then spits you out either stronger or a broken mess. It's a dance with death, and the prize is those moments of pure thrill, a perfect lap, pushing the boundaries of what's possible. Looking back, I wouldn't trade those years for the world. It made me who I am.

Gurney, Rain, and a Lucky Sweater

I get this offer to go drive for Ferrari – yeah, Ferrari. The Nurburgring's coming up – I'd kinda mixed up the order of those races – and I'd been on this testing streak. One of those cars was a full-on racer, the kind you can't just walk into a showroom and buy, you know? Every day, I'd hit the track, have lunch with Enzo and Americo – who spoke perfect English, thank god – and they'd just pump me for how the car felt, my reactions, the whole nine yards.

Then bam, outta nowhere, Tonner, my manager, calls: 'You're in! Nurburgring!' I'm like, 'Cool, who's car?' He says, 'Ferrari, I guess. Yeah, definitely Ferrari.' I go 'Right, so what's the game plan?'

I mean, I know this track is nuts. 130 corners? You can't memorize that monster, especially since it's 13-and-a-half miles long. So I tell them, 'I need a week's head start. Get me a Peugeot, anything, and just let me drive the circuit for a week straight.' Thing is, I couldn't get it into my head. Honestly? Halfway in, I wanted to go home. It's a week out, cars aren't even shipped, and I'm telling Hans, 'This is insane. I can't do this.' He just keeps going, 'Relax, you'll be fine, all good...'

Then the race cars show up and boom – big circus time. Factory teams everywhere, the whole shebang. That's when the pressure really starts to cook.

Okay, they tell me the Nurburgring is a thousand kilometers, one driver starts, one driver ends, then some dude hops in the middle – championship race, the real deal. Guess who gets the middle slot? Me. Whatever, no problem, right? This Belgian champ or whatever is handling start and finish. Cool with me.

Thing is, I get in the car, and suddenly, it all clicks. Like, a whole three-mile section makes sense. Right gears, right lines – the whole damn thing. Suddenly, those 13 and a half crazy miles, they're not so crazy anymore. Feeling good.

Last day of practice, I'm out there hustling. Coming round the carousel - that banked turn? Scary as hell - I head up the hill. Then this guy waves a blue flag. Means 'move over, hotshot coming through!' Problem is, I'm in a GT car, figure it's faster to blast through this corner than slow down. I dive in, full throttle, trying to be outta this guy's way and – BAM!

Lotus. Upside down. Back against the wall. Nose in the air. Back then, no seatbelts. So the driver's just hanging there, and I'm headed straight at him. Gonna be a head-on smash. I lift off the gas, crank hard right, floor it, come outta that mess sideways. My heart, I thought it'd stopped. Scared myself silly. Pull into the pits, people are sprinting my way, all these languages I barely understand. I hop out, Hans is walking up, I'm like, 'What the hell is happening?'

They're all yelling, 'You broke the record! Von Trips' record, the GT lap!' I'm thinking, 'Jesus, let me try again, I spun out there!' But Hans, he puts his hand over my mouth, says 'Not a word, just walk.' Couldn't make sense of the crowd buzzing around me.

Next morning, at breakfast, I bump into some Americans. Clark Gable, maybe, or guys I knew from California racing days. I'm sipping coffee, race starts at 10, it's maybe 8:30, 9ish. I'm telling them how I'm driving that middle stint, how I broke this record... they're all pumped up. Gotta hit the bathroom before the madness starts.

Mid-stream, this Ferrari mechanic bursts in. By now I get enough Italian to understand – they need me in the pits, like, right this second. I'm like, 'Sure, lemme just finish up here. '

Down to the pits I go, and what do they tell me? 'You're pulling double duty, starting and finishing the race.' Great, right? Now, this is a true story – back then, they lined you up and boom, you sprinted to your car. No fancy safety belts or harnesses in those days, hadn't even been thought of. Just you, rattling around in that coupe like a loose nut.

So there I am, lined up way down the grid with everyone else. Countdown's in German, you gotta understand. They get to four – I'm a young pup then, 22 years old – and I hear these footsteps coming, then a voice: 'Marshall Hawthorne, you bastard.'

The crowd thins, I'm still standing there like a dope. It's like trying to cross Sunset Boulevard to the beach – on the busiest day of the year. That was the start, man. Bumper-to-bumper, barely easing on the gas to keep from smashing into the guy ahead. God, what a mess.

Now, the way the Nurburgring's laid out, you pass the pits here, then kinda double back behind them. So even by the first lap, the guys would have a board out, try to signal you. Well, as I zip by, they're all quiet, just waving me down like 'Easy, kid, ease up.' But hey, I figure I've got a rhythm going, right? You don't want to break that, so I push on.

Lap after lap, they keep up with the 'Slow down!' signs. By the time I come in for the driver changeover? We're miles ahead of those Porsche boys that figured they'd dominate the whole thing. Miles. Turns out my co-driver stacks the car during his stint – no worries there!

But hey, that's when the Le Mans talk starts, 1958. They want me to partner up with Pedro Rodriguez, and you know what I say? 'No way. Forget Pedro.' See, by then, I had some pull. People actually listened to me. So long story short, that's how Gurney gets the Le Mans ride.

They're scrambling for drivers, and someone – can't even remember who – asks if I know anyone decent. Now, Dan… Dan Gurney's this California hotshot, pure Riverside Raceway, right down to the tan. Guy probably never saw a cobblestone street in his life, let alone those twisty European circuits. But something about the kid, I dunno… he just had that look in his eye. So, I go, "Yeah, I got a guy. Dan Gurney'll do it."

Cut to a few weeks later, and this lanky kid steps off the plane in Paris. Looks like he hasn't slept in days, which is probably true. I've got this old coupe – a real gem, mind you. Won the Tour de France a couple of years back, an honest-to-god Ferrari. Problem is, by the time I got my hands on it, the thing was more rust bucket than race car. Rain? Forget about it, you were wetter inside than out. But it's all I've got to show Dan the track, so off we go.

Night falls as we pull out of the garage – and I mean pitch black out there on those Le Mans backroads. No streetlights, just these pathetic little headlights that wouldn't help you find a lost poodle. Picture me, hunched over the wheel, squinting like I'm eighty, while Dan's in the passenger seat looking like he might puke any second. Rain's coming down sideways too, just because the universe has a sense of humor.

We finally pull up to the hotel, and wouldn't you know it, Old Man Kennedy himself is on the porch, probably sizing up the new talent. Dan goes to get out, and the whole door handle comes clean off in his hand. I'm not kidding. The look on this poor kid's face – it was a mix of horror and "Did I just make the biggest mistake of my life?" I just clapped him on the back. "Welcome to Ferrari, kid," I grinned, "At least it's not raining inside anymore, right?"

Well, wouldn't you know it, that junk heap ended up a rocket ship. See, the Ferrari guys, those engineers in their crisp suits with all their notebooks and calculators? They got all up in our faces during practice. Car ain't fast enough, they say. Our lap times? Lies, apparently. Now, me and Dan, we're arguing back. This thing feels like a slug, we tell 'em, doesn't matter what your fancy stopwatch says.

Turns out, they'd messed with the carburetor settings before Le Mans. Don't ask me why, these Italians had their own special kind of crazy. But once we put things back the way they were supposed to be... holy smokes. We flew! And that's when they drop the big bombshell: run top ten by midnight, you'll be top five by the checkered flag. Dan looks at me, I look at him, and we both get that same glint in our eyes. Enzo Ferrari himself rarely came to Le Mans unless he smelled a win, and those engineers didn't joke about things like that.

Thing is, about Dan Gurney… you gotta know he wasn't like the rest of us. He was in that rare breed – the Mosses, the Clarks, the guys a whole level above the competition. They got some extra spark, some magic that just ain't fair for the rest of us. Guys like that, they aren't just good – they're brilliant every damn time they strap themselves into a car.

So that '58 race, that was the start of the whole crazy ride, a testament to guts, a beat-up Ferrari, and the sheer talent of Dan Gurney. Sometimes, you just gotta throw caution to the wind, you know?

So, Canetti – this bigwig Ferrari engineer, always dressed to the nines – he sits us down, Dan and me, and starts this whole long-winded speech about the Mulsanne Straight. Now, this thing's legendary, right? Four miles flat-out, with this little kink at the end. We're talking 170 mph in those days, which may not sound like much now, but trust me, in those glorified tin cans, it felt like lightspeed.

He's going on like, "Remember boys, when you're on that straight...blah blah blah..." Dan and I are exchanging side-eyes, wondering where the heck this is going. Then the guy drops the punchline. He tells us this story – and I swear it's true – about how he's flying down the Mulsanne one year, glances down, and realizes he's forgotten his fancy watch. The expensive kind, he says, and he's just moved to Paris, so he's picturing this watch sitting on his piano. Now, mind you, he also mentions that he suspects his maid's a thief... so his brain's already in a weird place.

Dan and I are staring at him, wondering if the man's lost his marbles. Then Canetti goes, "I'm so wrapped up in this whole missing watch thing, I look up and Bam! I'm at the end of the straight, flying way too hot for the corner."

Now, in those days, there's this cafe right at the edge of the track – tables outside, big hay bales for protection, the whole deal. Canetti goes on, describing it all in vivid detail, right down to the spilled drinks and startled patrons as he plows right through the hay like a runaway bull. Finally, I can't hold back. "Hang on, hang on," I interrupt. "What happened in the race?"

"Oh," Canetti says, like it's no big deal, "I won the thing."

Dan and I burst out laughing. This old-timer's pulling our leg, right? But he's dead serious. "Here's the lesson, boys," he says, all stern now. "Mulsanne's the only place you get a break in this race. Don't go to sleep, but don't let your mind wander either." Then he just pats us on the shoulder and walks off. "Got the message, sir!" we call after him, still chuckling.

So yeah, add that to the list of crazy stories from those days. Speaking of crazy, '58 turned out to be the rainiest Le Mans on record. Nineteen straight hours of downpour – you couldn't see a darn thing. Anyway, with all this going on, the start approaches. Dan and I worked out this strategy around that whole "finish tenth - get fifth" promise the team made us. We figured, hey, let's just see what happens.

They stick Dan in for the first shift - those were some long stints back then, three, maybe four hours. Limited too, so you gotta pit on schedule or else you're out.

Rain. That's all I could hear as I strapped myself into the cockpit, the rhythmic drumming drowning out everything else. It had started a sprinkle during Dan's stint, but now it was a full-blown deluge. The pit crew kept hovering around me, this plastic sack of roasted chicken like some kind of unwelcome mascot. "Hungry, Bruce?" they'd ask, their voices muffled by the rain cascading off the roof. "No thanks," I'd mumble, my gut churning with nervous anticipation.

I was wearing my lucky Sebring rain gear – a ratty old ski sweater that I swear held some magical power. But honestly, all the luck in the world wouldn't help if this car broke down in the middle of Mulsanne Straight. There wouldn't be a soul out there, not even a farmhouse to beg for a sandwich. Finally, with a resigned sigh, I snatched a drumstick. Nowhere else to put it, so I shoved it under my sweater, right against my chest. Talk about unconventional on-board snacks.

Dan tumbled out of the car, a face full of rain and a grimace that spoke volumes about the track conditions. "Bruce," he wheezed, "It's like driving on ice out there!" Great, just what I needed to hear.

Visibility was the real killer. The downpour reduced the track to a blurry mess, the headlights carving out a pathetic, fleeting tunnel in the swirling darkness. One moment I was battling for position with a hulking Aston Martin – Shelby himself behind the wheel, I thought I recognized him – and the next I was lost, the world a swirling, watery vortex.

RACING IN RAIN is hazardous as Bruce Kessler learned. Shortly after this photo he crashed and burned Ferrari.

The pitboard signals were useless at high speed. You only got them coming out of the Mulsanne kink, a slow corner where the crew could hold up their signs. This time, though, the rain smeared the board into an illegible mess. Panic started to gnaw at the edges of my focus. I couldn't read my signal, but salvation came in the form of the Aston. We were neck-and-neck, trading positions like seasoned duelists. This might not tell me my lap, but it did tell me something crucial: the general position of the race.

Hours blurred into one another. Nightfall began to paint the sky a bruised purple, the rain still a relentless drumbeat. I knew I was somewhere in the top five by this point, the fifth or sixth hour ticking by. Time to pit, I decided. Better safe than disqualified.

As I roared down the front straight, I caught another detail – the Aston had disappeared, likely in the pits for a scheduled stop. That was my cue. Flicked on the blue light, the signal to my crew that I was coming in next lap. A backmarker D-Type Jaguar, a lapped car already out of contention, sputtered around the Dunlop Bridge just then. Perfect, I thought, plenty of space for me to come in.

But wait. As I looked up again, a green light beckoned from the pits. The green light that meant the D-Type wasn't out of the race after all. The green light that might mean...trouble.

Something's wrong. The car feels off under the Dunlop Bridge, and the rain suddenly shifts, flowing unnaturally, like the track itself is rebelling. Then, up ahead, I see it: a flash of silver on that slight uphill bend, the D-Type I'd passed laps ago now sitting sideways, half off the track, smoke billowing… and as my eyes adjust, the pit lights hit something at the top of the hill, something metallic.

But the green light, it's still on. That's when the steering gives out. I'm skating on something, on aluminum I realize, a piece of the D-Type shredded across the track. I'm careening toward the wall, the same wall they put up after Le Vay's crash, and everything inside is screaming. Fuel's low, the car could explode… My only option is to try to angle onto the grass, try to control my crash landing, if such a thing's even possible.

They say I was doing 120, but it might as well have been light speed. With everything on the line, I jump. For a fleeting second, I think I might get away with it. But as soon as I'm airborne, I know I've misjudged everything. My body, it's a ragdoll out of control, tumbling and thrashing against the wet earth. Luckily, I avoid landing headfirst, but everything else – my ribs, my legs – scream in protest as I finally roll to a stop, half on the track, half on the grass.

Nothing works. I can't move a muscle, all I can do is stare up at those spectators perched along the wall like hungry vultures. I'm waiting for them, for someone to rescue me. But the green light must still be on, because no one's moving. That's when the chaos erupts. Cars start piling up down below, a chain reaction fueled by misinformation. Panic courses through me – if I can't get off the track myself, what chance does anyone in that wreckage have?

United Press International Photo

The Ferrari of Californian Bruce Kessler burns furiously after it had rammed into the wreckage of a Jaguar near the Dunlop bridge. Kessler recovered from serious injuries, but Belgian Jag driver Jean Brousselet died.

LEMANS

Finally, it's over, and the spectators clamber over the wall, rushing towards me. One guy, an old RAF pilot, he speaks English. "Are you alright?" he asks, again and again, and all I can reply is, "Nothing works. Nothing."

The ambulances, they're all tied up with those other crashes, the results of this downpour from hell. They manage to rustle up some beat-up pickup truck, toss me in the back, and drive me not to some high-tech medical center, but some little countryside chapel where the nurses are all dressed in full nun habits. Talk about surreal.

TRAGIQUE CARAMBOLAGE AUX 24 HEURES DU MANS

Le Français Mary, télescopé sous la pluie par l'Américain Kessler, se tue à 200 à l'heure

And those nuns, well, they don't waste any time. They're out of stretchers, so they find a darn door, plop me on it, and wheel me inside. I'm about to find out just how out of place a Californian racer can feel, because the next thing I know, some priest is trying to give me last rites. "Hey, hold on!" I manage to yell. "I ain't going anywhere yet!" Of course, with the language barrier, it's a lost cause.

Then, the real fun begins. They start doing what they do to accident victims – cutting off your clothes for a better look. That's when I finally get stubborn. I won't let them touch my sweater, my lucky Sebring sweater. No amount of shouting and pointing seems to help until it finally dawns on them… unzipping will do. They peel back my rain jacket, then the sweater, exposing my chest. And there, amidst the grime and rainwater, are the remains of my pit-stop chicken, splattered all over me. You should have seen the looks on those nuns' faces!

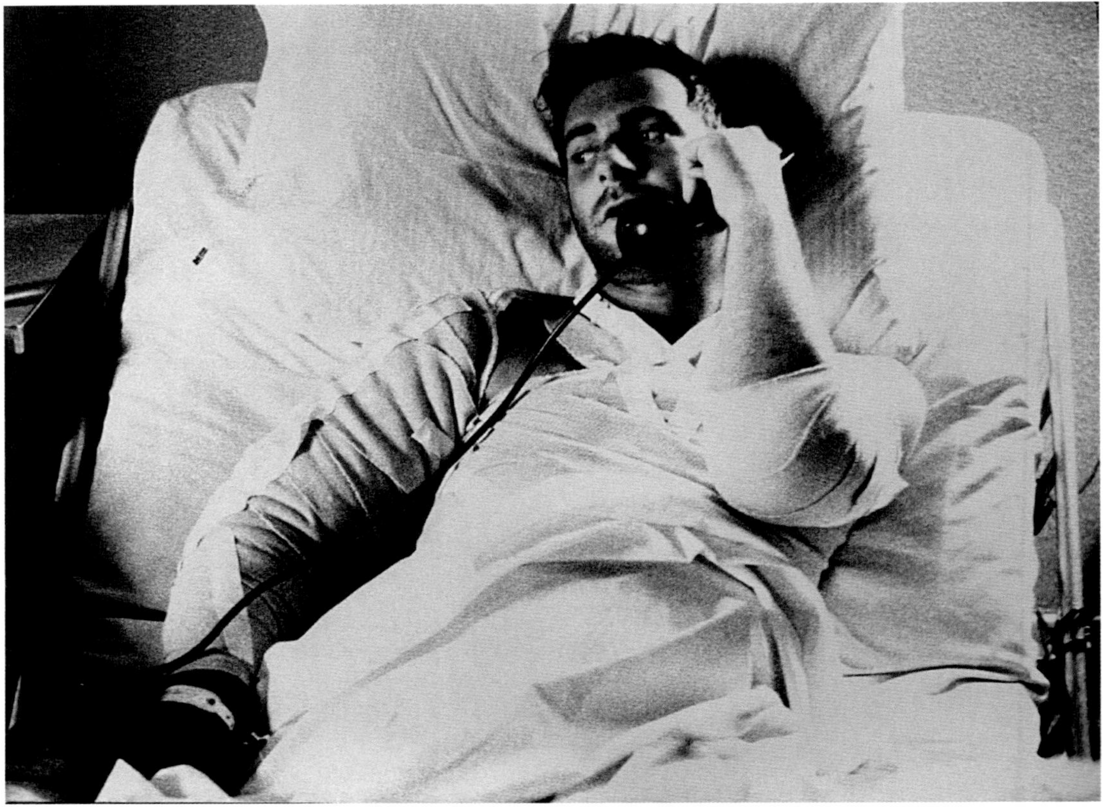

Back at that tiny French hospital, it's a full-on circus. I can barely breathe, my ribs are on fire, and what's the first thing I see when they pull back my sweater? My demolished dinner, spread across my chest like some kind of twisted Jackson Pollock painting. "No, no!" I manage to gasp, "It's chicken!" Honestly, you'd think I had a third head growing out of my shoulder the way these nuns were staring. One of them even fainted on the spot.

Turns out, the whole chicken saga somehow made it onto TV. Like, national American primetime TV. The Johnny Carson show, of all places! I should explain, my buddy Kurt Newman, a producer type, had connections to Carl Reiner – you know, the comedian. They were gonna have me on the show, and knowing they'd want a good story, I shared the whole chicken debacle with Reiner a few days prior.

Now, get this: Carson himself can't make the show, so they tap Reiner to take over. My jaw hit the floor when Reiner goes on and tells my chicken story, word for word, like he'd been there himself! Then Skitch Henderson, the bandleader, pipes up. "Bruce!" he says, like we're old pals. The whole thing was a trip.

You wouldn't believe it, but that single night made me a minor celebrity. Mom said the phone never stopped ringing. All because Carl Reiner was kind enough to share my near-death, chicken-splattered experience with America. Just another bizarre twist in the crazy life of a racecar driver, I guess!

From Le Mans to 'I Do': Lance Reventlow

So, get this – the Le Mans car Dan and I drove in '58? Turns out it was the very first Testarossa Ferrari ever built. See, that's why some rich collector shelled out 16 million bucks for the thing years later. Wasn't about me or Dan, it was just a piece of automotive history, you know? Kinda crazy how those things work, huh? That whole story's in the Wall Street Journal – some article they sent me, nice of 'em. Anyway, enough about cars... what else should we dig into? Jump back a bit, maybe we can stir up some of those Hollywood stories about Lance... you know the ones.

See, Lance wasn't your typical Hollywood type. Not by a long shot. So, him marrying some actress – Jill St. John was the name – well, it certainly got some tongues wagging. Oh, and we're talking to Jill, right? Hold on, Cheryl Holdridge? Nah, man, we gotta get the story straight from the source. Anyway, you know how they met? Lemme tell you...

It was '58, I'm almost positive – had to be. I'm over in England, prepping for some race or another, and Lance starts sending me these gushing letters. Telegrams too, he always had a way with words, even if he did go a bit overboard sometimes. All about this fantastic new girl, how she's nothing like those typical Hollywood types, how she isn't out for the fame and using him for publicity... Lance always was a romantic, bless his heart. Well, wouldn't you know it, next thing I see in those London tabloids, there's Lance and Jill, painted all over the gossip pages. Hmm, guess he was wrong about that publicity stuff.

But hey, they ended up getting hitched, so guess I was the one out of touch that time. Jill... well, she was Jill. Had a fiery spark to her, and I'm glad she and old Bob Wagner found each other. Talk about an unlikely pair! But seems like a good fit, at least that's what Bob tells me. Done a ton of shows with him, always a riot on set. Besides, Bob finally settling down? That's got its own chapter right there.

Jill's probably busy penning her own book, dishing all the behind-the-scenes stuff. I'll leave those stories to her. Anyway, back to the good stuff... See, I don't recall Jill being with him in Nassau. But she married Lance right in the middle of our racing days, sometime after I'd traded my helmet for a producer's chair. They did the whole thing quietly, practically a secret elopement. Fancy hotel room in San Francisco, with the only witness being Barbara Hutton, Lance's eccentric heiress mom. Now, that's what I call a one-of-a-kind wedding!

So, Lance ended up marrying Jill. That was after our time down in Nassau, sometime in '59 or maybe '60. They did the whole thing quietly, I believe... just in some fancy hotel room in San Francisco. Barbara Hutton, Lance's eccentric heiress mom, was the only witness. My mom always joked that she wanted Lance to marry a nice Jewish girl, but Jill was definitely second choice – or third, I don't know. Anyway, Jill, she was around during those later racing years. Remember the trip to Australia? That was when things started to fall apart.

Lance picks me up straight from the airport. Calls me, tells me to meet him at the Lua – you know, that old Hollywood haunt. Sits me down, looking real serious, and says he's done with the marriage. Jill was on the plane with him, and the whole flight home… well, let's just say it wasn't a pleasant trip. Asks me what he should do, and I tell him – there's only one option, really. He needs to talk to Jill, lay it all out clean, and get his lawyer, Stan Mullen, to handle the details. But Lance, he looks at me and says, "I just can't go on like this, Bruce."

I still don't know exactly what went down on that flight, but that was it. The beginning of the end, right there. Shame, really… they were only together a couple of years, maybe three tops. But hey, Lance was never one for that whole Hollywood scene. Him marrying an actress, even one like Cheryl Holdridge, well, that was just one of those things, I guess.

Speaking of Cheryl – and weddings – lemme tell you about Lance's real wedding, the one with all the photos and hoopla. We're getting ready to shoot Redline 7000, my office right down the hall from Hawks'. His secretary calls up and says there's some hotshot stuntman-slash-race-driver asking about a role, something to do with cars. I tell her he's got the right guy, send him on down.

This good-looking fella walks in, real confident-like, talking about being a race driver and wanting in on this movie. Asks what kind of racing we're talking about, and I tell him it's NASCAR, all stock cars. He starts backpedaling, saying he's a sports car kind of guy, and I ask him what he drives – Austin-Healey, Triumph, that sort of thing. "Where'd you race?" I ask, and he rattles off a bunch of local California tracks. We're going back and forth, and I get this feeling… so finally, I ask, "Ever heard of a little race called Le Mans?" You should have seen his face! Then he goes, "Well, I guess you must know Lance Reventlow."

Of course I knew Lance, dammit! So, I tell him I'm going to Lance's wedding – the big fancy one – and wouldn't you know it, this fella says he's invited too! Starts talking about maybe carpooling, and I'm thinking, no freaking way. Finally, I lay it on him: "I'm not just going to the wedding, pal. I'm the best man!" Shoulda seen his face drop. Now that, my friend, is a true story.

A Whole New Kind of Sports Show

My buddy David Sontag – now let me tell you, this guy has some luck. You remember that whole plane-in-the-Hudson River deal a few years back? Miracle landing, Clint Eastwood made it into a movie, the whole nine yards? David was there, last seat, last guy to walk out alive. The captain, he checks back, says all clear, and there's David. I told him he could've auctioned his underwear on eBay, made a small fortune!

But way before that, when David's still a young hotshot PR guy, we're talking out here in LA, working with Hilly Elkins. Hilly was a character, became a big-time producer. Anyway, David works his way up the studio ranks, ends up running the show at 20th Century Fox for a while. But back then, he's landed at ABC, on the network side in New York. Well, the bigwigs are whining about their Sebring coverage on 'Wide World of Sports'. You remember those days – live cameras, cutting between four sports every hour, and Sebring? Dull as dishwater.

David, though, he's in one of those exec meetings, probably a junior guy back then, and he gets this glint in his eye. Tells them, 'Hold on, fellas, I've got something to show you.' And what does he put on? 'The Sound of Speed', my movie! These suits, they flip. They eat it up. Thing is, they don't get it's a real movie, see? Scripted, staged, the works.

Next thing I know, David's on the phone. I'm between pictures for Howard Hawks at the time, so I say 'Sure, what's going on?' Turns out, ABC wants me, bad, because of that movie. David tells me 'Take the flight, they want to meet you.'

So I fly back east, walk into this meeting with the network suits. They're still gushing – 'Your film! Incredible! We want you to do Wide World of Sports!' I have to hold back a laugh. I'm like, 'Guys, that was cinema. You're live-action. It's a totally different animal.' But they're insistent. Then they bring up Sterling Moss, the narrator. Turns out, even Sterling thinks it's the greatest idea ever – loves my movie, says I know everybody in racing, I won't ask dumb questions, that whole spiel.

At this point, I'm looking at David like, 'What have you gotten me into?' Finally, I tell them, 'Alright, here's the deal. You're live TV, right? I'll shoot this whole thing on film, edit it, and you can air it next week.' Amazingly, they go for it!

"Alright," I say, trying to keep a straight face. "And who's gonna shoot this shindig for me?" Figured these suits at ABC had no clue what goes into making a film.

Turns out, they think they're covered. "We got a whole crew!" they tell me. "Guys that do all our NASCAR stuff! Eighteen cameras, whatever you need!" I just nod. Okay, sure, why not give it a shot?

So off I go to Sebring, and wouldn't you know it, first person I run into is Augie Pabst. He sees me, face lights up like it's Christmas. "Thank god you're here!" he bellows. "Need a driver!" This is starting to feel a little too familiar...

"Augie," I say, "Love to help, but I'm a director. Director Schmechter - rhymes with Wrecker," I tell him, can't help but throw in a dumb joke. "You won this thing, you drive." But no, he won't take no for an answer. I finally wiggle out of that one, barely.

Next up, Sterling Moss arrives, and we give the drivers the pep talk. I tell 'em, folks know me from racing, so this won't be like the usual 'Wide World' nonsense. We're doing it different. They all nod along, and I ask Graham Hill to get things going. I figure, hey, let's roll the car out, Sterling will stroll over, ask him what he's driving... Simple, right?

But Sterling, bless his heart, opens his mouth and the first thing out is: "Graham, world champion, what are you driving here today?" Graham looks up, deadpan, climbs out of the Ferrari. I follow him, camera rolling, as he walks around, stares down at the badge like it's some alien creature, and says, "It's a Ferrari, I believe."

That's when I knew. This whole thing, it was gonna be wild, the likes of which nobody'd ever seen on that show. And the best part? Because of Sterling, I had access to everything. The drivers' meetings, you name it. Now, Ken Miles was running the Cobra team back then, and let me tell you, this one meeting... Ken's laying down the law: no reckless driving, no mistakes on the first day, all that jazz. Well, wouldn't you know it, an hour later I hear whispers in the pits: Ken's just smacked his Cobra into a hay bale, car's banged up good! They tell me he's got it hidden away in a Ford hangar, trying to bash it back into shape with a sledgehammer.

"No kidding?" I say to the guy, trying not to grin. So I grab Sterling, and we both know what's up. We sneak in with the camera, but I've had them rig a blanket over the lens, can't see a thing. Sterling walks right up to Ken, "What's going on here, Ken?"

Ol' Ken, he stammers out, "Ran into a bloody hay bale..." and Sterling cuts him off, dead serious, "Yeah, I heard you laying down the law earlier. No messing about, anyone gets reckless and they're out... " Miles starts to sweat. You see him realize he's caught, starts looking around, figuring out who blabbed. But our camera? Blinded. He has no clue. He ends up offering to help Sterling fix the thing!

All of it went to air, I tell you. That kind of behind-the-scenes stuff nobody'd ever seen on 'Wide World'. Me talking with Roger Penske, Sterling chatting him up... gold.

We even did this whole piece on a Ferrari pit stop – now, I practically wrote the script for this one beforehand – and Sterling comes in later and lays down the narration. I tell them, "You could get better service at a gas station!" Watching those guys bumble around, arguing... that's television, right there.

But the real kicker? The way we finished that show? Back then, ABC had these big editing studios, either Pittsburgh or Philly. Massive rooms, and I bring in like four editors, work 'em day and night. We're all practically sleeping there. Never worked like that before, writing bits of the show as we go along, then Sterling comes in and lays down his voiceover.

I'm cutting, adding music, all of it... I even put that march from 'Bridge on the River Kwai' in, you know the one? They had this rule where a mechanic couldn't go out to fix your car if it broke down, but a driver could go back to the pits, grab parts, and fix it on the track. So I have this bit of Voight walking across that bridge, and I use that music as the driver's hauling parts back out to his car. Stuff like that, nobody'd ever done on sports TV before."

So I figure, how am I gonna kick off this film? Decided to start with a night shot – race ends at 10 pm – the winning car, lights on it, but you can't quite tell which car, who the drivers are. Big, wide shot, the whole nine yards. Minute the race ends, I send guys out to take photos of dented cars, broken parts, all that aftermath stuff. So my movie opens with that, and Sterling's voiceover: 'You're looking at the aftermath of one of the greatest races in the world... stick with me...' Then we cut to the car, but it's a mystery, right?

I wrote the whole intro for Sterling, practically handed him the lines. Anyway, show 'em the film, tell David my plan... oh, everyone gets excited. Then it's Saturday, the show's going live in, what, 15 minutes? David gets this call. I hear him on the phone 'Yeah, I know it's got music... No, wait, we discussed the opening... What do you mean? This is ridiculous! We can't air this!'"

At this point I'm sweating. Figured I just got David fired, and what a way to go out. But then he says, 'Well, what else are we gonna do? Show's on in 15! We're stuck!' My friends and I, we're all glued to the TV, excited as hell. And boom, there it is – the whole show, exactly how I cut it.

We're rolling on the floor laughing, loving it. Then the phone rings. David tells me head honcho at ABC – and I swear, his name escapes me right now – wants me in his office Monday at 7 AM sharp. Now I'm really kicking myself. My flight back to LA is Sunday, but they've changed it, no questions asked...

So Monday rolls around, bright and early. I walk into this bigwig's office – guy's got a name, everyone knows him – half expecting to get the axe. He looks up, and says,

'Kid'. (And yeah, I'm still just a kid, 23, 24 maybe). He says, 'Never in the history of this network, any show, have we gotten the reaction we did for yours. The audience ate it up!

They loved it! Head of ABC offers me the world on the spot: 'Stay, kid! Produce, direct, write, any show you want. There's this new thing, 'American Sportsman'... it's yours.' But what do I say? 'Sorry, sir, gotta get back to Hollywood. Gotta do my own thing.' David, of course, ends up a bigshot, runs 20th Century Fox for a while – total success story. Those breaks, you know, the way things fall into place... Funny how it all works out.

Speaking of which, credit goes to David for setting me up with Joan. He's in PR, see, and I tell him about working on this Elvis movie, 'Roustabout'... I spot Joan Freeman walking across the Paramount lot, ask who she is, that whole deal. Then that night, flip on the TV, and there she is again, on some show called 'Bus Stop'. Twice in one day!

So I'm chatting with David, he's asking who I'm seeing, and I tell him – kinda playing it cool – 'Nobody special, but I saw this girl, Joan Freeman... wouldn't mind taking her out.' I swear, he must have pulled some strings - studio PR guy and all - because next thing I know, I'm on a blind date with her!

She's living with her folks in Burbank, so I hop in my VW – hey, gas was cheap back then – and that's how it started with Joan. Anyway, David, he's still around, retired in New Mexico or somewhere like that. Great guy, had a fantastic career.

How 'The Sound of Speed' Got Made

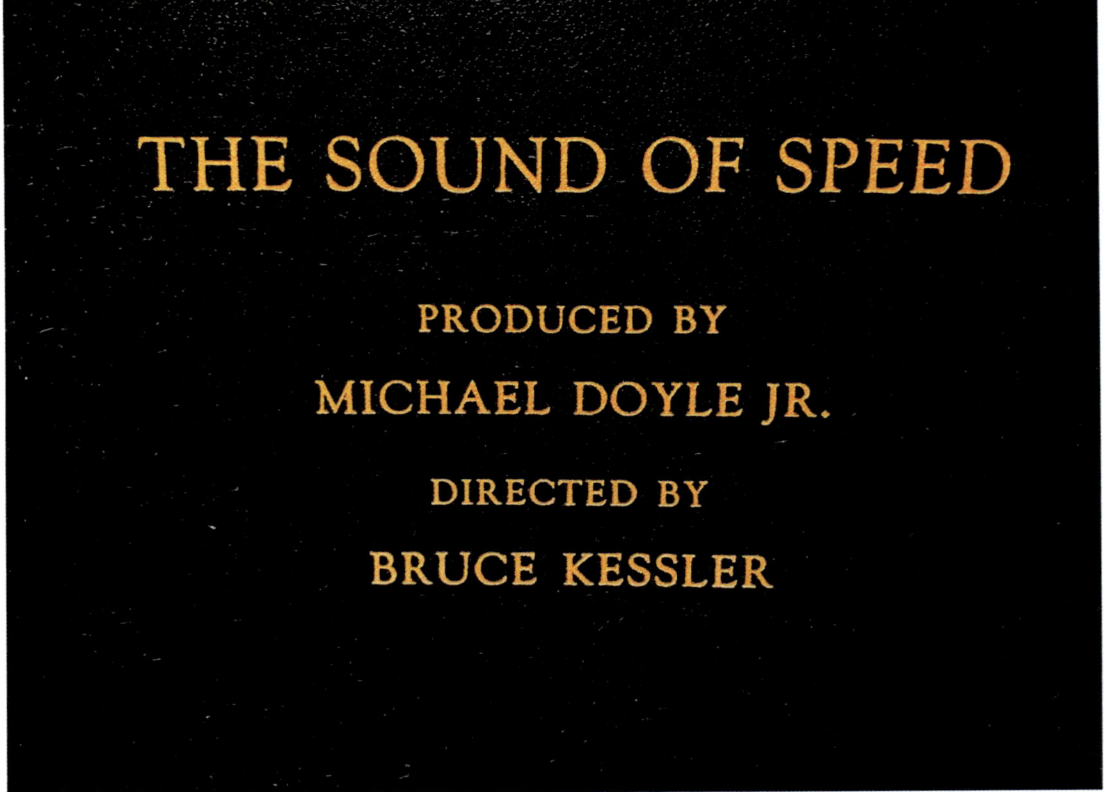

So there I am, a technical advisor, and the next thing you know – poof! – I'm a script supervisor. All thanks to some guild mix-up I didn't even understand. MGM gets in some hot water, and suddenly I'm responsible for this whole shoot with stock car footage... which yeah, I basically directed, but they spin it so I'm the script supervisor. I didn't even know what that was!

But hey, it gets me in the guild. Turns out they couldn't make me an assistant director, but script supervisor? Sure, why not. Anyway, I end up out at Lime Rock for this. Go to the script supervisors' guild, and Thelma, the head lady there, takes one look at me and says, 'Kid, you couldn't take shorthand if your life depended on it!' And let me tell you, she wasn't wrong. I literally had to write the whole damn alphabet down the side of my script so I wouldn't mix up the shot numbers.

But hey, you learn on the fly in this business, right? Jumped through some hoops, ended up apprenticed, and wouldn't you know it, I forgot where I was even going with this story! What were we talking about? Oh yeah, 'The Sound of Speed'...

Right, so now I'm an apprentice script supervisor. Land on this set, 'Studs Lonigan'. Got a real script supervisor, thank god, and the cameraman is Haskell Wexler. This guy, Chicago fella, all he wants to talk about is racing – which okay, I get it. But the studio's so uptight about him they literally hire two cameramen! One shoots the movie, the other sits around twiddling his thumbs just so Haskell can do his thing. Talk about Hollywood, right?

Anyway, I'm watching Haskell, see, and this dude's a genius. One day, he's dancing with the lead actress, borrowed her boyfriend's jacket, got it slung over his shoulder... and then suddenly he whips out this little wind-up camera and starts shooting close-ups of her. Right in the middle of everything! No dialogue, no setup, just this beautiful woman, and him making it look like art.

Cut the scene, and I'm like, 'Haskell, could I stick a camera on a race car?' He barely looks up, says, 'Sure, kid, knock yourself out.' I ask about maybe using an Arriflex, since those hold more film than those wind-up things, and he's all for it.

So I go home, buzzing. Figure, why not tell Lance Reventlow my crazy scheme? Well, I lay it all out for Lance – Haskell, the Arriflex, my big idea for a racing movie – and Lance, cool as ice, just looks at me and says 'Let's make a movie.' The thing is, we ain't even got a script!

He thinks for a second and says, 'Okay, how about a short film?'. Still no script, mind you. Then he hits me with, 'How about that short story you wrote, what was it called... 'Huey Must Die'?' Turns out my high school journalism teacher got so weirded out by it, she'd called my mom!

So Lance, he starts laying down the law: 'I'll give you the car, the crew, I'll even help out, anything you need. Just gotta find the money for the film, and oh yeah, one rule: no talking, no narration.' Real generous, right?

But hey, a challenge is a challenge. So I mull it over, figure 'Yeah, I can make that work.' And off we go! First up, making a camera test. We take that single-seater Scarab they built for me, slap a Chevy engine in it... oh man, you're gonna see some amazing shots we got! There's one real famous one, me in the car, just sitting there smoking, thinking who knows what.

So, we rig up this Arriflex camera in the Scarab. Head out here to Venice, just a block west of Lincoln where our shop is. Stick Chuck Daigh in the car, ready to give it a test run. Now, we'd heard this record, 'Sounds of Sebring', so we track down the guy that made it, lives somewhere out in Riverside or San Bernardino... Anyway, we ask him how he pulled it off, and he tells us, 'Nothing to it! $45 Japanese tape recorder, that's all.'

So we say, perfect, but we gotta stick it in the car. He warns us, gotta put the mic in the driver's pocket, muffle it a bit or it'll be all engine noise, and we do just that. We buy the recorder, put Chuck in the car one afternoon, stand by the road, and off he goes!

I'm shooting it with this 13.5mm lens over his shoulder, so you can read the gauges, see everything. And Chuck, he's really wrestling the car, throwing it into corners, sideways, the whole nine yards. We want to get some real excitement on film, you know?

Send it off to Consolidated, that's our lab. Standard stuff, they develop overnight, so we head in around noon the next day to see our dailies. Walk into the room, and wouldn't you know it, there's a bunch of suits in the back row... Lance, me, Warren, maybe Chuck was there too. Figured they're just curious, tell them 'Sure, have a look!'

Lights go down, the film rolls... and you see all of it, the real deal. Lights come back up, we're all pumped, and these suits, they're baffled. 'How did you do it?' they ask. I'm like, 'What do you mean? You just saw it!' They insist, 'But how did you make the film?' And I finally tell them, 'Look, we just did it, that's what happened, you saw it!' They think I'm pulling their leg.

But hey, we knew we could pull this off, shoot right from the car. Of course, then came the real problems.

You know, sometimes a little ignorance is a good thing. If I'd had any sense, I probably never would have attempted this whole crazy plan. But that's kinda been the story of my life, hasn't it? Just jump in and figure it out later.

So there I am, trying to work out how the hell I'm gonna film this car going 180 miles an hour down at Riverside. How do you keep up with that? No way you can get a camera alongside it, no equipment like that exists. We're talking 1959, maybe '60 – hell, maybe even '62, who remembers?

Anyway, I end up at Armsteads. That's the place over by Goldwyn Studios in Hollywood, the pro place, where you rent serious gear if you're making a real movie. Not some homebrew thing like we're doing, nobody shoots 35mm amateur!

So I explain my problem to them, and they tell me, 'Hey, we got these crazy lenses, the kind only Hughes Aircraft uses. Think like a 500mm or 1000mm, something huge. They stick 'em half a mile back to track takeoffs, that's the only way to get the shot.' Tell me it's a real pain to use, needs a special mount, the whole bit. But hey, maybe that could work!

So, I take Mike Murphy, who was my camera assistant, and I make him the cameraman! Then I go out, hire what other guys I can find, and off we head to Riverside to see if this crazy lens idea would even work. First attempt? Well, you mostly see my shoes, a bit of the track, and every so often, there's this tiny glimpse of a car half a mile away – that you're supposed to be right next to! Clearly, this wasn't going to be easy...

So I get in some real pros. We head out there again, talk strategy, and I finally figure out a way to at least keep up with the cars, not have them just be little specks. Gotta work on holding the camera steady from a distance, make it feel like we're bringing the car to you, all that stuff.

Right before we're about to start shooting for real, two things happen – and yeah, this whole story gets kinda twisty, so bear with me. Somehow, I scrape together the money for the film. Don't ask me how, I couldn't tell you now. But these backers start making demands – maybe we gotta have Jill St. John in it, that kinda stuff – and of course, me being a creative genius, I toss the money back at 'em.

That's when I end up going to George Burns. Remember, grew up with him and Ronnie, best buds, roomed together... Ronnie tells me, 'Go talk to my dad, he makes movies all the time!' So I pitch it to George, and he says, 'Alrighty, I'll back it.' That's how we finally got financed.

Now, here's one of those weird little side stories that always seem to happen... I'd met this woman, Marjell DeLauer. Used to be married to Bob DeLauer, pro football player for the Rams. Well, she became a literary agent, goes to this Hollywood party full of big shot directors. Somehow Howard Hawks gets to talking about wanting to make a racing movie, and Marjell pipes up: 'Oh, I know a guy! Used to be a driver, he's making one right now!'

So Marjell, she gets a little associate producer credit, all because of a party conversation. And there I am, sitting in this tiny office at General Service Studios – George Burns owned that whole lot – with nothing but a chair, a desk, and a whole lot of hope. The phone rings, and wouldn't you know it, some lady asks for Bruce Kessler. I say it's me, and she says, 'Howard Hawks.' At first, I figure it's gotta be some buddies from the track playing a prank, right? But then there's this soft voice, and it says, 'I hear you're making a film...'

I tell him yes, it's about a race car, about this one driver... He asks when and where I'm shooting, and would it be okay for him to come watch. Now, I'm still half-convinced this isn't real, but I figure I'll play along. So I say, 'Sure, Mr. Hawks, come on out!' And you wouldn't believe it, there's that classic photo of Howard just over my shoulder, watching me film.

Well, he watches, and you know, I'm all fired up. Laying out the picture for him, showing him my script. Next thing I know, he turns to me and says, 'What are you doing this weekend?' I say 'Nothing, sir', and he invites me out to his place in Palm Springs, says he wants to talk. Figure, why not?

So I head out there, and he starts in about how all these filmmakers today, they're all New York writers, living in their apartments, they don't know a thing about the world, about life and death. I'm just kinda nodding, not wanting to argue with the legend. Then he says, 'You, you get it. You understand what it means to be on that edge.' I say 'Okay', because what else do you say when Howard Hawks tells you something like that?

He really lays into it, says he wants to work with someone who knows what it's like to be on the edge of life and death, not these New York guys who never set foot outside their apartments. Starts telling me all these wild stories about his racing days, back when they had the old Beverly Hills board track... you know, right where that fancy Hilton stands now? Tells me he had his own sprint car, and about this rival driver guy, a real tough customer.

One race, this guy pulls the dirtiest trick on Howard, so Howard gives it back to him tenfold, sends him flying through the fence. And wouldn't you know it, someone brings Howard a photo of this guy flipping off the camera mid-crash! And Howard just looks at me, dead serious, and says, 'How can you not like a guy like that?' I'm like, 'Yeah, of course!' And just like that, him and I, we're buddies. Crazy how things work out, huh?

When a Legend Opens Doors

So the next day, Howard tells me this story about this photo, the guy flipping him off as he flies through the fence. And Howard, with that drawl of his, he says, 'How can you not like a guy like that?' And all I can think is, 'Yeah, that's pretty awesome...' Turns out, this whole time Howard's talking about his old camera guy, and him and I, we're getting along because I just got divorced too.

So this guy moves in with me, and we become buds. One day I ask, 'Hey, he's gotta be a cameraman now, right? Maybe we've worked together.' And then, Howard – that deadpan way he has of talking – goes, 'Oh, no... He went on to become a director' I'm figuring, maybe I do know this guy, so I ask, 'What were some of his movies?' And he just says, 'Gone With the Wind'. That's how it happened, I swear.

So I end up going to work for Howard after that. He makes Paramount put me under contract. But you know, how often does something like that happen in life? And I made sure Marjell got that associate producer credit, since she put the whole thing together. Now, later on, when I finish the film, the whole thing with it almost getting disqualified happens... falsifying the release, like we all did back then with short films. Paul Newman was one of the other directors!

You see, we'd all put our films in release for a week, just long enough to qualify for the Oscars, and then figure we could up the price once it was nominated. Well, that year the Academy gets all up in arms, says we falsified the releases, disqualifies the whole lot of us!

So I'm stuck. Got this film, no clue what's gonna happen with it, no plan at all. Then one day, I get this phone call, 'Go get the trades, read 'em.' I'm like, 'What am I looking for?' 'Just go get the trades!'

So I do, and I'm flipping through, can't figure out what this is about... and just as I'm about to give up, I see it: 'Sound of Speed, best U.S. short film, going to Cannes'. I almost fell over. Couldn't believe it!

Right away, I'm on the phone to Goldwyn, to Billy Wilder's... I talk to his secretary, Rosella – must've been a hundred years old, sweet lady – and ask if I can see Billy. He says sure, so I run down to Goldwyn, burst in the door, and there he is. Billy Wilder, cigarette hanging out the corner of his mouth, practicing puts.

So I go charging into Billy Wilder's office, right off the bat he looks up at me and – in that thick Austrian accent of his –says, 'Well, now you can go home and tell your mother you're an artist!' Honest to God, that was his opening line. All I can do is sputter, 'Billy, what do I do about Cannes? Should I go, should I stay?' See, I know the film inside and out, but festivals, that was all new to me.

And Billy, he says, 'You have to go, Bruce. Just to see what it's like. After that, you can make up your own mind.' That was classic Billy Wilder, always the pragmatist. But you know, he was a huge help on this film. Doesn't get talked about much, but it's true.

For months, while I'm deep into the final cut, I'm hauling myself over to Billy's office with 'The Sound of Speed', begging him, 'Please, I need you to watch this.' And him, straight as an arrow, he tells me, 'Bruce, I'll watch it. If I don't like it, I'll never tell a soul I saw it. And if I do like it, I'll shout it from the rooftops.'

So we run the film. And after, he says there's only one problem: 'You know what this film is about. Maybe those racing guys do too. But nobody else does.' I go into my whole spiel about no dialogue, no narration, those were the rules... And he cuts me off, says, 'That's not a problem! We can fix that easy.'

That's where the intro text comes from. I sit there, scribble it out – 'You are listening to the heartbeat of a Grand Prix racing car' – something like that. 60-some years later, and that little phrase is stuck in my head. That was what the film needed, see? That, and Billy getting me to write it down, not try to explain anything else. He said, 'Just put it on the screen, let 'em figure it out.'

So that's a big part of how 'The Sound of Speed' got made – me and Billy, arguing over a film reel. And of course, there was the relationship I had with Howard Hawks... Honestly, just having his name behind me? It was magic. If I said I was his second unit director, nobody cared what else I'd shot!

Opened every door, made everything so much easier. But him and Billy, those two... there's a whole book in their stories, I swear. You'll see one in mine, about Howard Hawks, guaranteed to make you laugh.

So, years later, Bogdanovich – the guy that did 'The Last Picture Show', among others – he's working on this book about Howard Hawks. He tracks me down, and I'm in it, but what he's really fixated on is how did I land that job, right? I mean, looking back, I got that – he's still starting out, trying to figure out how this whole industry works...

That's how I got started, all luck and circumstance. Anyway, he throws me back in, needs that one line, 'It paved the way for me.' What was it in full? That working for Howard Hawks... yeah, that's it.

'Working for Howard Hawks, anybody would accept you. They automatically knew you had to be top notch to work for him.' See, back then, as his second unit director, Howard was 70. I thought that was ancient! 'The old man', we'd call him. Now that I'm 84... well, that's a whole other story.

Thing was, Howard would get tired, right there on set. Shoots a master shot, starts the scene coverage, then it's three in the afternoon, and he turns to me: 'Bruce, finish this for me.' And without missing a beat, I'd say 'Sure'.

Not that it was hard! I knew the scene, understood what he wanted. So that's how I started actually directing, little bits here and there. He'd take a breather, and I'd just... pick up where he left off. Evolved into it, really.

A Friendship Forged in Speed and Legacy

Lance and I, we both had asthma, see. That's why I ended up out at the National Asthmatic Foundation, used to be called Brandes School, down in Tucson. Lance was at the Southern Arizona School for Boys. See, down there, folks ended up with all kinds of allergies, that's why the schools existed. First time Lance and I meet, it's 'cause the schools were playing some sport or other.

And wouldn't you know it, we got to talking cars. Our mutual passion. Thing is, he didn't get hot rods, and I saw no point in some stuffy Jaguar sedan. Just seemed useless to me. He wanted to know what good a hot rod did... so there we are, two young guys arguing cars, and that's how we became pals.

Later on, after graduation – I'm working for Warren at this point – Lance comes out to California. His mom sets him up nice, house overlooking Universal Studios... even had this houseboy, Dudley Walker. Picture perfect servant, right out of central casting!

Anyway, Dudley finds me at Warren's shop. Lance had told him about all of us – Sonny Balcain (you'll be talking to him too), Wally Green... later he'd be this bigshot writer, Waylon Green. And there's Jack Russell, this older guy, ex-paratrooper, handlebar mustache and all. We called him Handlebars.

Well, Jack comes up to me, asks if I know anyone in the movie biz. I say not really, and he tells me this wild story: He wrote a heist story between jumps, thought it could be a film. Called it 'Ocean's Eleven'! So yeah, whenever that franchise pops up, look real close, and you'll see Jack Russell's name.

For years he'd drift in and out. Always needed a few bucks, claimed he'd been to Tahiti, that he'd helped Michener with his next big book. I figured he was full of it, but check the forewords on Michener's stuff – always thanking Jack Russell. One of the strangest, most interesting guys you'd ever meet.

So Lance and I, we pick up where we left off. He spends most of his time at my parents' house, where we had this huge dining room table. Didn't matter who you were – friends, car guys, random folks passing through – Lance liked having dinner with the family, they just sort of took him in.

Now, Warren and Simone, they nurtured me as a driver, that's how we ended up together. He saw something in me, convinced me to try Formula 3. I wasn't super keen, but Warren said it would make me a better overall driver, help my career... So we become partners on a car. Think I owned the engine, he had the chassis, something like that.

We had this JAP engine, no clue what the initials stand for, and at first, I didn't know much about any of it. But then we're up against the Formula 3 crowd, and the moment I start racing... I start winning. Folks start flocking to Norton Engines. Warren tells me to make the switch, and of course, we keep right on winning. The car was amazing, and that's what kicked off Lance's racing career – which I've talked about before, how the Mercedes came into the picture.

When he decided to get serious, we figured a 1100 Cooper would be a good starter car. Funny story about that, Von Dutch and those pinstripes – remember, I told you about having to mask them over at Elkhart Lake? But anyway, that whole time, Lance really becomes part of the family.

Jumping ahead a bit, after I got hurt at Pomona, Lance didn't want me racing anymore. When this movie gig came up, and I told him about Haskell, about how we could shoot from the car... Lance really pushed me to go for it, to leave racing behind.

That's what led to 'The Sound of Speed', to my whole career, which I guess we've covered a bit of. Lance and I, we stayed close through it all.

Now, there's this other piece – I'm gonna jump around, but it's all about Lance… I'm not sure how old I was, the year's easy to find because it's the year he died. I'm out in Hawaii, scouting for a pilot. Lance is living there, so I crash with him, and he's the healthiest I've ever seen him. Surfing all the time, just looked fantastic.

When I'm done, I tell him I'm off to Europe to film 'Assignment Vienna'. I say, 'Why not come with me?', knowing he doesn't like Europe. He says no, like I expected, and that's that. So I head off on that film. Bob Conrad and Joe Campanella – names I came up with, by the way.

You know, shooting a movie is a whole circus, especially when you're on location somewhere like Vienna. Grand sets, rolling Austrian hills... a big ol' production, is what it was. Well, one evening I get back to the hotel, room buzzing like a beehive with missed calls. Ten of 'em, at least! Cheryl, my mom, some friends... my stomach flipped when I saw Cheryl's name first – back then, she was married to Lance.

So, I bite the bullet and call. It hits me like a ton of bricks: Lance. Plane crash. Aspen. I'm numb. Turns out, everyone's calling to tell me the same awful thing. Then Cheryl's on the line, bless her heart, and she's in a fix. His mother wants the body shipped back east, the whole family plot thing. But Cheryl KNEW Lance wouldn't want that. Aspen, that was his place. What should she do?

Well, I told her straight-up, "Lance would want his ashes scattered there, Cheryl." It felt right, you know? She did too, but time wasn't on our side. I knew if she didn't act fast, his mother would get hold of the body and that'd be it. So, I said, "Cheryl, grab some folks. Cary Grant – he was like the only father Lance ever cared about – and a few others." She was a trooper, even in her grief, got 'em together.

Next day, I was on set, but my head... it wasn't there. Shock, I guess. Did this big, complicated scene – troops marching, crowds, a whole spectacle. I'm usually on point after a take; tell everyone why we're going again, what needs tweaking. This time? Cut! Nothing. Dead air. Finally, Campanella – sweet guy – pulls me aside. "Bruce, what was wrong with that? Looked perfect to me." And I just say, "I don't know, I didn't see it." Blank. Just blank.

That feeling lingered. Days went by in a fog. Then, Cheryl pulls the whole thing off. Now, there was some... fallout, let's say. First off, she gives me Lance's car. Beautiful '16. Me? No use for it. I say, "Donate it to Briggs' Museum." Later, well, that car becomes a whole mess. See, Cheryl remarries, not-so-great guy, needed money... he sells the car, even though it wasn't his to sell. She apologized about that till the day she died. Bless her, I scattered her ashes out in Santa Monica Bay myself.

Other things went missing too, like Lance's scrapbook. Shame about that. Priceless stuff in there, memories... but hey, that's life, right? Things happen. You lose people, you gain some. And some of those memories, the good ones, you carry 'em with you always.

Funny how things work. Years down the line, that scrapbook of Lance's, it resurfaces. Now, that kind of thing, it's not about owning it. It's history, pure and simple, and it belongs out there for folks to see. And damn, looking back on that whole situation, Cheryl... she handled it like a champ. Five days, that's all she had. Get those ashes to Aspen, gather a few of us who meant something to Lance, people important to him and me... Shame I can't recall all those names now, mind like a sieve at my age.

Cary Grant, though, that much is clear. He stepped right up, helped her through the worst of it. Ah, Lance... so many memories flood back, even now. We were inseparable, him and me, from way back 'til I got caught up in the movie business. Brought a whole new world, but it didn't change how I felt about him. Folks used to think I was his bodyguard, always ready to jump up if someone looked at him the wrong way, cracked a joke at his expense.

Now, I might've mentioned this before – hanging out with Lance at that coffee shop, Lenny Bruce used to rib us when we first started going there. "Bodyguard" this, "bodyguard" that... then he finds out I'm from a well-off family and suddenly it's "two little rich kids." Lenny always had a way with words, that's for sure. Interesting times, growing up in that crowd, let me tell you.

Inseparable Paths: Bruce and Lance

You know, me and Lance Reventlow, we were thicker than thieves back in the day. We didn't go anywhere without each other. Dinners at my folks' place, hanging out after a long day at work – we were a package deal. You couldn't find one of us without the other, that's for sure.

Looking back, those were the golden years. Motor racing was in our blood, see? Especially with the Scarabs. Oh man, what a ride that was. See, if you'd asked me back then what I was gonna do with my life, I'd just have shrugged. 'Race car driver,' that's all I wanted to be. I couldn't picture anything else.

The Scarab, now that was something special. Started as a wild idea over in England with Brian Lister, then boom! This incredible Formula 1 car started taking shape. The crazy thing is, that Formula 1 dream, it got crushed. Lance, bless his heart, couldn't get the parts, the machinery he needed. Everyone was too swamped. We even tried building our own engine – remember those desmodromic valves? – but it was no use.

By the time all that went down, I'd moved on. Still, I was always around, watching Lance fight tooth and nail to make that Formula 1 car go. We even tried an international three-liter, with an Offenhauser on gasoline, but the horsepower just wasn't there. Thing was a tank, let me tell you. Only ever drove it once, just to get those tax write-offs. We knew it was a lost cause.

Problem with that big old three-liter was it just wasn't built for the times. You needed something smaller, lighter – a Maserati with a birdcage frame, that was the ticket. But hindsight's 20/20, right?

Me and Lance, we stayed tight 'til the end…well, almost. He sold the house he built when we were barely 20. Things were different then, you know? But hey, that's life. Sometimes you go one way, sometimes another. But those Scarab days? Man, those were something else. The guy was barely older than me, just a month and a day, and what does he do? Builds himself a whole damn house at age 20! We called that place Camp Climax, and let me tell you, it lived up to the name. We had some wild times out there, the kind you never quite forget.

Years later, he sells Camp Climax and moves up into one of those swanky canyons – Benedict or Coldwater, always get the two mixed up. But through it all, Lance and me, we stuck together. Hell, even Wally Green was in the mix back then – Waylon

Green, rather. Before he hit it big with that gritty Sam Peckinpah flick... darn it, always forget the title, but it was a doozy.

See, those early years, we were inseparable. That only changed when this whole directing thing took off for me and I got swamped with work. Lance, he starts heading out to Hawaii more and more, falls in love with the place. Brings over this monster of a beach cat, a proper 40, maybe 50-foot beast. Made quite a splash down at the Marina Del Rey, let me tell you – no one had seen anything like it.

Even with that boat, it feels like yesterday. Must be 50 years ago now... man, time flies. That thing was pure speed on the water. Even managed to snag ourselves a speeding ticket, clocked at 20 knots right in the marina! We stayed pals, don't get me wrong, but it wasn't the same. Different lives, you know? He's living the island dream, and I'm stuck back here in the Hollywood grind, even doing those overseas shoots.

But right before that awful accident in Aspen, fate throws us a curveball. Studio sends me to Hawaii, of all places, and who do I stay with? Lance! Damn lucky break, getting to spend that time with him before... well, before it all went wrong.

You see, Lance was a pilot, born and bred. Could fly anything with wings, a certified weather-rated, multi-engine pro. Which makes it all the more tragic – him being stuck in the backseat of some dinky little plane, flown by a student and instructor who get disoriented and smash right into a mountain. Lance at the controls? That never would have happened.

Lance was very Nordic and he looked like a Prussian soldier and he walked like one. I almost had to run to keep up with him, but his personality was amazing. He was, for as erudite as he may have looked, he could fit into any conversation, whether it was outlaw motorcyclist, Hell's Angels, or if it was with fancy politicians. Let's face it, he could charm the socks off anyone, put them at ease in a heartbeat. Not at all what you'd expect from a guy with his background, right?

He could adjust and be at ease with anybody, in any situation. And he was also great at putting other people at ease. He was not at all what people thought he might look like he would be. He walked and talked with authority, but behind it all, Lance had this way of making everyone feel like they mattered, like he was genuinely interested in hearing what they had to say.

He was a terrific personality and extremely, how would I, I guess flexible. You could put him anywhere and he would fit right in. He was great.

Of course, it's tough having a mother like that. And his mother, of course, was not around. I mean, I've only met his mother on a few occasions, a very limited number of occasions.

She kept places, she kept a bungalow at the Beverly, at either the Beverly Hills Hotel or the Bel Air Hotel. I'm not sure which one, Beverly Hills probably. And when I say she kept it, nobody could use it. She may not be there for a year. She kept a place at one of the hotels across from the pier – it might have been the Ritz – in New York. And operated under the same situation. Couldn't use it. Only Lance could use it.

And Lance and I might stay, you know, in one of those places. And she did the same thing in Paris. I'm trying to think of the name... I think it was the Hotel de Paris in Monte Carlo. I can't think of the name. But one of the major hotels right on the square, she did the same thing in Paris.

She was, how should I say it? A woman who would... she was very attractive. But she was, lived in a very unrealistic lifestyle. She was surrounded by hangers-on, hanger-on people. People who were trying to take advantage of her, wanted to be around her. We were, I was uncomfortable around her. And Lance would try and get me to go with him sometimes, particularly when he had to go see her, especially if we were looking, if he was looking to negotiate something with her. But it was hard to get her alone because all these hanger-over, hanger-on type people were always around her. I really don't want to say too much about her. The book, Poor Little Rich Girl, is a very accurate description of her. There's, of course, a picture of Lance and I in it together.

But there are stories I will not talk about that happened, but in my presence. I just don't feel it's the right thing to talk about.

As I say, we were, you know, we were inseparable. And so, to understand Lance, I think I explained him pretty well when I said he could fit into any crowd. He could be comfortable with any crowd and he could diffuse any situation. If a group of outlaw motorcyclists came in and because they knew he was rich and so on and started to pick on him, he could diffuse him. Or I'd be jumping up to defend him. And they'd be eating out of his hand by the time they left. His personality was that way. He could deal with anybody. He was great.

It's hard for me to talk about him because we had a relationship that was different. We were not like...how would you say it? We were not like good friends. We were just kind of inseparable at that time in our lives.

So I have a hard time talking about him. It actually makes me feel like I want to cry when I dig back into the past and remember this person who was that close to me. It goes beyond your typical buddy, this was a deeper connection.

Can I ask, you came back and decided to build your own car, the Scarab. What led to not just one car but building several of those? Well, I've talked about this earlier. You have how we talked about it when we talked about the Preston Lerner book. We've also talked about building the first car in Warren's apartment, when I sat there and described how I thought the car should be built.

Those decisions to build a second car, first, a second, and a third car, came from Lance and Warren and the plan to build a team of cars, instead of just a single car. I'm sorry that I cannot give you the accurate information on how that decision was made. Even though I was there, I really can't remember what triggered the decision to build a second and third car. Except that we decided, or Lance decided, that we were going to run a team, a three-car team. That was what led to building car number two, which was the five car.

That was the Chuck Daigh car, the car number three, which was my car, to be my car – but turned into the third car, after which it was, I went on to drive for other companies. I came back to drive the car, I did drive the car in competition... There's a lot of things that happened in that period of time, it's all a bit of a blur now. But I will tell you this:

After we ran that three-car effort the first time, those cars had barely been started before we hit the track. We had the Offenhauser in for those tax write-offs. When I talked to Lance afterwards, I explained to him that the car was not ready to race. I mean, we'd never really run the thing before that event! And of course, the engine was coming out of it right away, and a Chevy was going in.

Lance, I'd best say he kind of shrugged off my concerns. Figured I was being overly cautious, you know? When I said, "This car is not ready to run, you just don't fire up a race car and take it to the track," I think it went in one ear and out the other. We did okay with it on the racetrack that first day, which was frankly amazing.

But then he takes one of the cars out with that Chevy engine in, and he comes back absolutely furious with me. The thing is a deathtrap! Brakes, handling, it was all a mess. "This car is unsafe!", he yells…I just look at him and say, "Yeah Lance, guess you weren't listening when I told you this exact thing would happen."

See, cars like this need to be tuned, run-in, dialed-in... you can't just build them, throw 'em on a track and expect miracles. But anyway, so, you know, the only other time we really ran that car, which of course I talked about with the Riverside race – that's a story for another day.

But back to his personality… It was quite interesting. Lance, he had this amazing ability to fit into any crowd. He could just adjust and get along with anyone, put them at ease, no matter who they were.

The Final Laps of Friendship and Scarab

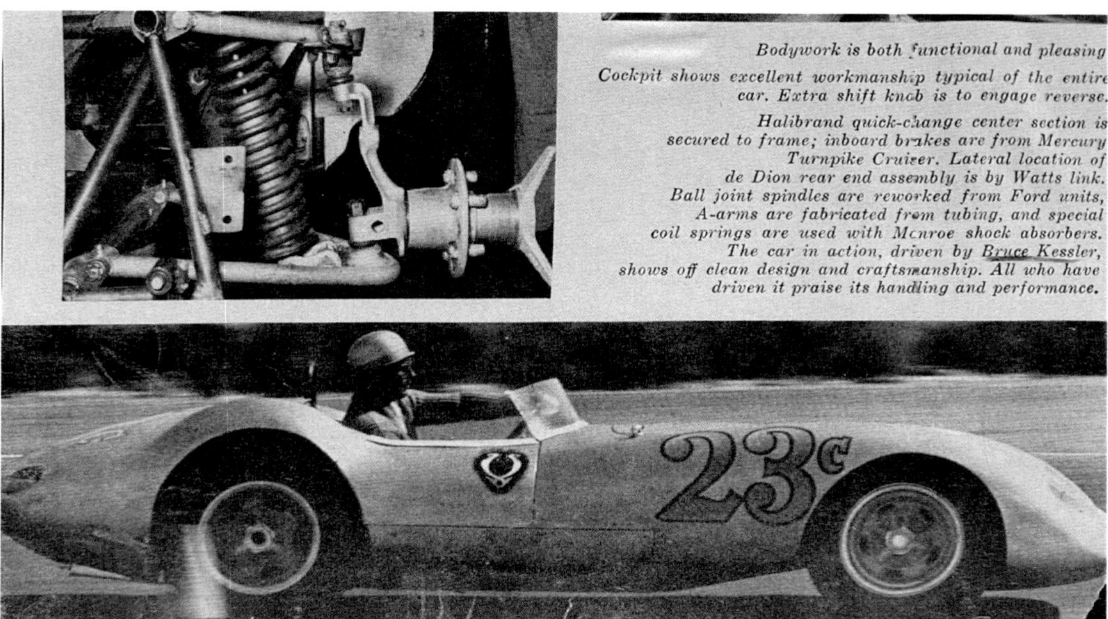

Bodywork is both functional and pleasing
Cockpit shows excellent workmanship typical of the entire car. Extra shift knob is to engage reverse.
Halibrand quick-change center section is secured to frame; inboard brakes are from Mercury Turnpike Cruiser. Lateral location of de Dion rear end assembly is by Watts link.
Ball joint spindles are reworked from Ford units, A-arms are fabricated from tubing, and special coil springs are used with Monroe shock absorbers.
The car in action, driven by Bruce Kessler, shows off clean design and craftsmanship. All who have driven it praise its handling and performance.

So, you want to know why I was behind the wheel of that Scarab in Santa Barbara? Well, let me tell you, it was a bit of a comedy of errors. The thing about Lance Reventlow, Chuck Day, Juan – the whole crew – they always had something in the hopper. Another race, another plan. This time they'd up and decided to haul off somewhere to the Midwest for another competition. Not that I blame them!

Left old me with a handful of guys – Sonny Balcano, I think, and probably Harold – and this car we were just getting on its feet. Lance turns to me, "Bruce," he says, "do me a solid. Run this thing, will ya?" Wasn't much of a question, was it? You gotta admire a guy like Lance, though.

Anyways, there we are, car's still half in pieces, but we get it on the truck. That's the reason Lance wasn't around.

Now, you gotta keep in mind, we're talking about three cars here. We start with the first... then how long was it before Lance goes and builds us a second? Then the third! It's a wonder we kept track of ourselves. After the first one was done, we break it in at

Phoenix, then Palm Springs. I wasn't around then, but from what I heard, things weren't exactly smooth sailing.

By that point, Lance and Juan, they'd made up their minds. We were going full-tilt, building out a team. I can't say I was there for those big decisions – heck, I was probably in Europe, hustling a ride for Canetti or some other outfit.

So, who's driving what? First car, well, that's Lance, of course. Second car they built, that was Chuck Day's. Number five. And the third car, the number three – that was for yours truly. And that was the Scarab team – right there.

Funny thing is, in '58, the year we really got those Scarabs rolling as a proper team, the whole year they were blowing everyone away – you know who was actually behind the wheel? Me, Lance, and Chuck. That's it. That was your Scarab team. Oh, and I was pulling double duty, running for North American Ferrari... anyone else who'd have me!

Of course, we had Warren Olsen, he was the man keeping the show on the road. Phil Remington, Harold Day on the wrenches... Chuck Day on the second car, me on the third. That's how it was, back in '58 when the Scarabs were at the top of their game.

You know, building those Scarabs, it was a whole team effort. Coons and Travers, they worked their magic on the engines. Then there's Troutman and Barnes, shaped those beautiful bodies. And of course, Chuck Pelley, the man who brought the whole design to life. That was the core of it all.

Now, there were others too – Raul, Sonny Balcain, I think he was with us in '58. Been a long time, hard to remember every face.

Then there's this interesting character, Ronnie Walrod. Don't know where Lance dug him up. Kid couldn't have been more than 16, 17. He was our go-to guy – coffee runs, errands, whatever needed doing. But he was right there with us, on the road with the team.

Funny thing is, years later, I'm directing this show, MacGyver. Got a boat scene that's giving us trouble, so I bring Ronnie in. Turns out, the kid's a natural with boats, big-time catamaran sailor. Well, we call him our 'boat wrangler,' but he ends up our maritime guy. Did a bunch of big movies after that.

Last I heard, he'd finally hung up his spurs, but made one heck of a living out of it. I think he was out in Arizona when he finally decided to call it a day. Just saw that anchor over his shoulder and figured that was that.

So yeah, Ronnie, another interesting one. Lance must have found him somewhere. We kept crossing paths – always good to see him, and him and Lance always stayed tight with that sailing connection.

Now, getting back to the cars… after we built those three, and Lance had his shot in F1, he decides to sell the whole team. It was the end of '58, and Lance figures the cars are done for, can't compete anymore. Nicky Chevrolet ends up buying them.

Here's the kicker – those Scarabs kept winning races for years! Lance was dead wrong about them being outdated. So yeah, a lot of folks know those cars as Nicky Scarabs, since they ran under that name longer than Lance had them. I'm sure you know they did the whole 50th reunion thing. Augie, I think he owns them all now. We were out at Elkhart Lake for the reunion.

And how about that 'Sound of Speed' car? The one with the Chevy engine, the one we used for the movie? Man, that thing's vanished. No clue what's in it now, or who even owns it. Might be a couple of them out there. England maybe? Sonny Raul Balcain, that guy keeps track of all that stuff. He'd know where they landed.

Thing is, industry was going crazy here in the States then. Lance couldn't get the stuff he needed to build his own engine – a real Reventlow, or Scarab engine. Don't even remember if it was supposed to have desmodromic valves.

See, those guys had the drawings, the whole plan. But man, things were humming here in the States, everyone busy. Couldn't get a team together, couldn't get parts on time... It's like, to build that engine from the ground up – blueprints, casting, everything – that was the big hold-up, that's how I remember it.

So, by the time they finally get over to Europe, those cars are yesterday's news. Front engines? When everyone's gone mid or rear? No chance. That's basically the story.

Timing was just all wrong. Took them forever to get those cars built, and by then, they weren't gonna cut it. Now, how many did they end up with? Two that made it to Europe, that's for sure.

Then there's the third – that 'Sound of Speed' car, remember? The one with the Chevy in it? That was supposed to be my ride if things had shaken out differently...

Man, getting anything done back then was a headache. Lance, he had a dream, you know? An all-American Formula One car. But the way industry was, he couldn't make it happen fast enough. So those cars, beautiful as they were, they were old before they even hit the track.

Now, did they build those first two cars together? I'm pretty sure they did... though hey, I was retired by then, so my memory's a bit fuzzy on the order of things.

I do remember photos of that third chassis, all by itself in the shop. Makes you wonder where the other two were hanging out. And where was this all happening? Right here!

Marina Del Rey, that's where we built those babies. Block off Lincoln, block off Washington, not far at all from where I'm sitting right now. Later on, Indy teams loved this spot too.

See, there used to be a shipyard nearby, big old building they'd take over, keep their cars in. Nice thing about that was being so close to the airport. Load 'em onto planes, easy as you please.

That was years later though. Point is, Marina Del Rey, Southern California, always a good spot for gearheads.

Okay, quick one – so, Scarabs fold, then boom, Shelby swoops in, right? Tell that story, how'd that go down? I wasn't in the thick of it, but here's the gist…

Well, after they came back from that Formula One adventure, Lance kind of throws in the towel. Not sure how things were money-wise, but in comes Carroll Shelby. Now, we all knew Carroll, been around the racing scene. This guy, he's got a wild idea – import those British AC Bristol cars, rip out the engine, slap in a little Ford powerplant...

He goes to Warren, goes to Lance, basically asks if he can crash with us while our team's winding down. Lance steps back a bit, but Warren, he takes over managing things for Shelby. Hell, Warren's the one who signed the whole Ford-Cobra deal for Carroll!

So Warren, he's right in the mix, all those guys we had, they become the heart of that first Cobra. Remember how they used to paint it with watercolors, change the color for photos so it looked like they had a bunch of cars? Well, that's another piece of racing history for you.

But yeah, that's how Cobra got its start, how Carroll got going. Ordered up one car, got one engine, and they'd watercolor that thing to high heaven. Meanwhile, Lance is out of the picture, and it's Warren running the show when Cobra kicks off. Even gets all the paperwork done with Ford.

Innovations, Transitions, and The Scarab to Sebring

So, Lance gets this idea – mid-engine car, right? Turns out that thing was a winner. Ends up getting sold to John Mecom, I think Freud drove it... After that, we take a stab at, what do you call it? A Formula Libre car. Sorta like Formula One, but with a V8 in it, if I remember right. Haul that thing all the way down to Australia, run it against the big boys, and do pretty darn good. That's the one and only time I remember that car getting on the track.

Now, what's going on with Lance's money at this point? I couldn't tell you. Taxes were a mess, that I know. And somewhere near the end, when the whole operation shuts down and Carroll Shelby moves in, I just know it didn't make sense for Lance to stay in the game. Taxes, other stuff, whatever it was... time to fold. Wasn't there some IRS thing too, tax laws changing? Look, I don't know the details. Wasn't part of that scene then, or maybe my memory's just no good anymore. Can't give you the play-by-play that led to the closing.

But hey, while all this is going down, guess who's turning into one of the most important guys in racing? Jim Hall.

I actually met the guy when I was 18, 19, maybe 20. He gets himself a Maserati 2-liter, same kind Lance had, and asks me to teach him how to drive it. Which I do, of course.

Turns out, Jim Hall, he's an absolute genius with cars. Ground effects, automatic transmissions, the whole nine yards. Went on to build this car, the Chaparral? You guys know that one. Changed the way the game was played. I'm about 84 now, and he's gotta be the same. One heck of an engineer, full of wild new ideas.

So yeah, he was one of those guys who put their stamp on the whole sport.

Okay, back to Chuck Pelley... you guys get him on board, he starts designing, all that. Was I involved much then? Let's just say they knew where to find me. I mentioned Chuck, how he came on board, all that stuff. Not much to add there. They narrowed the front end after I dinged it up, but that's about it. Chuck would show his plans to Lance, to Warren... don't think they asked for my two cents much. Hell, it was a long time ago.

But hey, I wasn't even around all the time. Lucky for me, I got to drive for other teams, go back east... that sort of thing. And those other teams, remember those Sebring photos?

Sebring, that's our big one. The only world championship sports car race in the whole US. Back in '57, Lance takes that 2-liter Maserati down there. Happens to be my birthday, which is how I remember all this. They wouldn't let me practice, Bill Pollack took my place. I plain wasn't allowed to drive. Don't think that car even finished.

But '58 – Ferrari, or really it was Canetti, asks me to drive. Teams me up with Paul O'Shea, great guy, national GT champ for Mercedes. That race had some wild stuff happen. Thing is, the car I'm supposed to share with Paul is coming from Italy too. It gets on the boat, but the race cars miss it 'cause they couldn't get them built in time. Turns out, that's the first time they ever flew race cars over to the US, instead of putting them on a ship!

So, things get even weirder – there's a shipping strike up in New York, and they can't get the car Paul O'Shea and I are supposed to drive off the boat! Canetti's desperate, so he goes to George Aarons, the big Ferrari money guy in the US – you know, North American Machine and Foundry – and begs him to lend us his 250 Berlinetta.

Now, this thing was a regular street car. Cigarette lighter, the whole deal. Nothing at all like the race car we were supposed to have.

So yeah, that's what we end up with for the race. We have to hack it up a bit, and with the Italian mechanics there... well, let's just say the language barrier was real. The rule is, lights on at 6 pm sharp, daylight or not.

We try to explain that to them, they rig something up, and there's a mark on the dash for 6 o'clock. Not sure if we even took the radio out, but this was a plain old street Ferrari, folks, and that's what we raced.

Not only do we win our division, but at one point we're third overall! Thing is, it's night, and I'm behind the wheel, and those lights are getting dimmer and dimmer. Clear sky, not a cloud around.

So, way out on the back straightaway, I kill the lights. Drive for a while, can see just fine. Long as there's no one behind me, I flick them on, they're bright for a bit, then start to fade again. I switch them off when I get clear... and they're calling in this mystery Ferrari running around in the dark. I mean, I'm flashing those lights when I come by the pits so they don't think anything's wrong!

Finally, they black flag me, so in I come. And you want to talk about arguments? World championship race, and I'm in the pits getting yelled at in Italian about the lights not working. Twenty minutes we're stuck there while they figure it out.

We end up winning the race, but all that pit drama drops us down to fifth or something. After it's all over, guess what? General Motors wants me to go to Detroit.

I just turned 22, I think, and here I am, this kid in a room with all these suits. They're grilling me about what went wrong for them, why we won. I'm just looking around like, 'Seriously guys? You were at the race. Your cars kept breaking down every few laps. What am I doing here?'

Kind of a funny moment, looking back. Now, I think I mentioned Curtis LeMay before? Always trying to get me to be a fighter pilot? Well, right after that race, right after the whole victory thing, he comes up and asks me again.

I say, "Well, I'd love to, but there's a problem." He goes, "What's that?" And first thing I say is, "I volunteered for the draft right out of high school. Got a 4F classification."

LeMay, he just shrugs. "Don't worry, I can handle that," he says. Then I tell him about my scholarship, being a former three-time Formula Junior champ, how I'm heading to England. Bruce McLaren, coming from New Zealand, all of that.

See, the thing he really wants is for me to drive for him. Thing is, pilots aren't drivers, and vice versa. I had to let him down. Still bumped into him later on, since he was friends with Howard Hawks, and all that.

Someone once said about Curtis LeMay, they should make a statue of him and put it under glass with a sign: 'In case of war, break glass.' Interesting guy, for sure. Funny how those connections get made, though.

When Directing Isn't on the Menu: How The Monkees Kickstarted My Career

So, I end up at Columbia, doing my technical advisor thing, then I'm a writer, then script supervisor... you know, working my way up the ladder. Talked about some of that before, how I got connected to Howard Hawks...

Anyway, one day I get this call from Columbia about doing a big second unit sequence for some major movie of theirs. Off I go to the lot for the interview. I'm walking across the lot when I get stopped by this young guy, one of my old assistants when I was script supervising. He's all excited, says he's off to ABC, gonna be some hotshot executive. Then he starts talking about this new show, The Monkees.

Thing hasn't even aired yet, but they've already sold it for a year. And he tells me, straight up, that if I'd take the script supervisor job, they'd give me a chance to direct the last episode in the run. I say, real nice of them, but no thanks.

I'm a director, see? Even if it's just second unit, same difference. Tell him thanks, but I'll make the appointment anyway. He says no, they don't want 'regular' directors. Now I'm interested. So, I tell my agent, we get the meeting set.

First guy I talk to is Bert Schneider. You know, the Schneiders owned Columbia, and Screen Gems was their TV arm at the time. Bert says, yeah, they know who I am. Then he says it's all up to his partner, who's right next door – Bert Rafelson. Talk about your Hollywood moments, right?

I go in to see Rafelson and the guy tells me – flat out – "We know you're good with action, but we haven't seen you handle people much. Can't take the risk." And there I am, walking out the door... when guess who I run smack into? Jim Frawley.

Now, I'd worked with Frawley before, back in my script supervising days. He's all smiles, "Hi Bruce!" Then tells me he's gotten his first directing gig. Asks if I want to do the episode. I tell him, no, they just shot me down. Frawley, he's a good guy. Says he needs help, will I be his script supervisor?

Okay, so I'm figuring, what the hell? When's the shoot? Turns out, I'm free. I tell him sure, I'll help out.

So, I go in, become script supervisor again. Now, here's the kicker – they tell me once you're back on the set as a tech, forget about directing. I mean, that's the Hollywood gospel. I tell my agent the whole deal, he's not happy, but I'm going to help out my pal Jim.

So, there I am, doing my thing, and who's directing the second episode? Bob Rafelson. The same guy who turned me down! He'd been keeping an eye on Frawley, so he says, "You want to stay on and help me too?" Sure, why not? I was free.

Well, I'm finishing up that episode, and I get called to the production office. Never a good sign, right? I'm figuring they're gonna fire me, something's gone wrong.

They say, "Look at the board." I'm staring at it. "What am I looking for?" Totally clueless.

It takes me a minute, but then I see it – my name, up next to start prepping. Turns out, I'm replacing Martin Scorsese. Remember, he's a no-name then, some kid from New York who got stuck on another project.

That's how my directing career took off. Word is, Jackie Cooper – big car racing fan, and head of Screen Gems then – when they showed him the list of candidates, he was all for me. Same with the editor on 'The Sound of Speed', who's running the whole editorial department by then. Apparently, when the vote came around, I got every single one.

So, I ended up directing four episodes. They told me, do a good job, and I'd get a show for the second half of the season. I did more than that, ended up alternating with the other directors. But right then, boom, I get my first movie offer. Started my whole new career.

What was the movie? Some AIP thing, Angels from Hell. Producer named Joe Solomon – did a ton of movies, that guy. I was replacing some director who moved on to bigger and better things. They picked me, mainly because of my action stuff, and I could shoot fast from doing TV. If I could handle that schedule, and they saw my action background, figured that was good enough. Joe Solomon, tough guy to deal with, to put it mildly. But hey, he gave me my shot.

Problem was, and this is where my agent and he went head-to-head, I hated the script. Had to do a big rewrite. Brought in a buddy, did a first pass, basically the same story Solomon wanted, but I just couldn't shoot his version. Title was killer though, Angels from Hell.

Funny thing is, when I see that movie on TV now, someone's ripped it off a TV screen, so the aspect ratio's all wrong. I shot it widescreen! But never mind all that, the movie was a hit, within budget, and suddenly I'm offered more movies, one after the other.

That's how I became a movie guy. In between, sometimes because I just love making stuff, I'd take on a TV show. But I got burned, let me tell you.

They change your movie title, make it something sleazy, misleading... that cuts deep. You spend six, eight months on one of these things. It's a piece of yourself, you put it all on the screen. At a certain point, just because I loved filmmaking, I decided enough was enough. I could work TV whenever I wanted, everyone trying to get me.

So, I did pilots, TV movies, you name it. Finished up in '97. I was burnt out, plain and simple. Had a little heart problem, and it all happened right during hiatus. So when they told me that, well, that made the decision easy. I'd been telling my management I was ready to hang it up anyway. They said fine, do it.

So yeah, in '97, that's when I quit. Got out of it all... It was during that break that I had the heart thing, which they took care of, no problem. But hell, I was glad to be retired. Done way too many pictures by then. That's the whole story. 1997, I decided it was time to go fishing.

Speeding Through Genres: A Director's Evolution

So, I'm prepping what? My second movie, I think... when a buddy calls me up, Friday night. Asks if I'm busy. Well, nothing major going on, so why? Apparently, there's this show over at Universal called It Takes a Thief, and they shoot their night stuff on Fridays so they can have the weekend for turnaround. His buddy wants to introduce me, so okay, why not?

Turns out they're shooting, I meet Robert Wagner, and I'm face-to-face with this guy Glenn Larson. Glenn's gone now, bless his soul, but this guy had history. He wrote music, led some band called the Four Preps, even wrote that song, 'Catalina Island, 22 Miles Across the Sea'... anyway, he's a rewriter on the show, about to be a full-fledged producer.

Wrote the script they want to give him to produce, has it right there. Bob's already going on about how great it would be if I directed. Before I've even read it, I agree, take it home, check it out. Well, I read that script, and I'm like, holy smokes, this is pure 1946 Warner Brothers. Peter Lorre, Sydney Greenstreet... you need those guys to pull it off!

Call up my agent, tell him how it is, and he basically says, figure it out yourself. So, I go back to Glenn Larson and say, "Look man, this is vintage stuff. Where are we getting those actors?" And without missing a beat, he says, "I got 'em."

Now, I'm thinking, did he raise them from the dead? But no, he swears he has a couple of guys who are spot-on. So yeah, we start pre-production. Six days. About day four, Glenn calls me, all in a panic. Apparently, the higher-ups finally read the script. They hate the whole 1946 thing!

I tell him, chill out, this is Hollywood. Go back, tell 'em you're doing a total rewrite. They'll calm down. They buy it, we shoot the 1946 movie anyway. Ends up a smash hit. He's a hero, I'm a hero, everyone's celebrating. Glenn, always joking with me later, says, "You did my first one, gotta do my last one too." Sadly, that didn't happen, but man, he went on to create a ton of shows. Look him up, you'll be amazed. One of a kind, that guy. That's how I got started in television.

Now, here's another one: Glenn comes to me, I'm at home, chilling out. Remember, no cell phones back then, none of that. Messenger shows up with a script. "I'm doing this show, McCloud. Fired the last director, you're the guy for this. Great sense of humor, the whole thing." Doesn't mean much to me at the time, but okay.

Messenger leaves, I read the script. Title was something like 'Horse Stealing on Fifth Avenue.' First McCloud they ever did. I love it! This whole bit with a New Mexico guy in the NYPD, horse gets stolen, that shot of him riding down Fifth Avenue – well, Madison, but close enough – just great stuff. So I sign on, and I loved that show.

Funny thing – well, maybe not so funny at the time – the lead actress, turns out I went to high school with her! Had nothing to do with me getting the job, mind you. She was already cast since they'd tossed the other director. I was just replacing him.

Anyway, I ended up doing what, seven of those McCloud movies? Dennis Weaver and I, we clicked on the set. No big social thing – never had dinner together or anything like that. Just a solid working relationship. Sometimes, he'd come up to me, kind of confused about a scene, not getting the joke. I'd break it down for him, and he'd say "Thanks, got it," and be on his way.

Dennis was a good guy, always meant well. Gave him my little lens finder one time when he decided to try directing. Never saw the thing again, but that's showbiz. Doesn't matter – I can eyeball it. Got this down to a science – this is a 40, this is a 50... anyway, I know that stuff inside out.

McCloud was my favorite show at the time. You look back over my career, there's so many... Mission: Impossible, Baretta... the ones everyone always remembers. But there's others that were just as fun, just as wild. Like Night Stalker... now that was written by this guy, David Chase. Can you believe that's the same guy who later created The Sopranos?

There was this book they wrote about great television episodes, and mine and David's episode was in it. Headless Hells Angel – the whole thing was a trip. David, I'd run into him before – never would have guessed what he'd go on to do, let me tell you. He was a good writer, though, always had that edge.

So yeah, in Hollywood, you meet a lot of people. Grow up around Beverly Hills, you're tripping over actors and directors. Like Robert Wagner – great guy, real sense of humor – that's how I came to direct all those shows of his. Even did a rare TV appearance with Natalie Wood once.

Speaking of 'RJ', we're on location somewhere I hate, complaining like a good director does. He grabs me by the wrist, hauls me a couple of stores down. There's an ice cream shop. Orders me a hot fudge sundae, tells me to chill out, everything's fine. The guy was pure class, knew just how to handle me.

He used to call me "The King" when I'd walk out onto the set. Turn to the crew and say, "Everybody bow to the King," and everyone would laugh. He was one of the great entertainers, loved by the crew, always joking with them. Just this incredible sense of humor, and a terrific guy to work with. Probably still is.

Natalie was a different kettle of fish. We went way back. In fact, I was there when Jerome Robbins was testing her for West Side Story... tough time in her life then, very different from how she ended up. Anyway, when she did that TV guest shot with me, I was the director, and some assistant tried feeding her lines. She turned on that guy, said "Bruce is my director, I'm doing it his way." Made my day, let me tell you.

I've had so many experiences, so many films. I was lucky, never stopped working if I wanted to, in television at least. Movies, they got crazy, and I wasn't having any of it. The only one that ever tempted me back was 'The Art of Racing in the Rain'. Took ten years for them to make that one! But hey, the guy who did it, I thought he hit it out of the park. Glad he made it, that's for sure.

But back to how I got started in television, well, Robert Wagner had a lot to do with that. I met him when I was working with Glenn Larson on It Takes a Thief.. you know, that was his first show as a full producer. RJ was there on the set, liked me, wanted me to direct... and that was it, off I went.

Lots of other shows after that, of course. You grow up in Hollywood, you're bound to meet everyone. Good people, mostly, though you have your stories. RJ, though... top notch, always had my back. Natalie, she was something else, bless her heart.

See, Natalie, she was having a rough patch then. Not at all like the girl I'd known for years. She'd gone through some changes, that's for sure. I think she was married to some English director at the time, not really sure. It just wasn't the same Natalie, not the bright-eyed kid I remembered, nor the star she became later, either. Still a hell of a performer, though, no doubt about that.

Anyway, I liked Natalie, especially working with her on that TV show. It was just a guest spot, but there's this one scene... has her, Eddie Albert, and RJ in it. Now, before they roll, you hear everything on those mics we're all wearing. The whole crew's wired up.

So Eddie, the script guy, he starts trying to coach her. Right there, on the mic, everyone listening in! She just turns to him, cool as you please, and says, "Bruce is my director. I'm doing it his way." I tell you, the whole crew, we were all grinning from ear to ear. I loved that moment.

Did the scene my way, of course! You work this long, you have stories like that for days. I've made so many films, been so lucky in this business. Worked whenever I wanted, mostly in television. Movies got too crazy for my taste. Only one ever tempted me back, and that was 'The Art of Racing in the Rain'.

Funny how that happened... this group calls me up, out of the blue. Ask me if I've read the book. I say no, but funnily enough, it's right there on my boat, on the coffee table. Turns out, someone left it there for my wife.

Well, I read the darn thing. Love it. Even tell them I'd come out of retirement for that project. This is years ago, mind you. Then they tell me Universal picked it up... and that book sat on the shelf for ten years! Typical Hollywood, right? But hey, I loved that story.

Guy who finally made it, I thought he did a bang-up job. I was thrilled with the movie. He did it justice. Wonderful book, and a shame it took so long for someone to see the potential.

The Director's Chair: Steering Stories and Managing Mayhem

I'm often asked, how do you go from being a race driver to a director? I don't know how to answer that question.

Being a director is you just tell everybody what to do. It's an easy job. You don't have to do anything. All you have to do is tell everyone else what to do. When I'm asked, how do I relate to actors? It's very simple. I read the script.

I understand what the actor's attitude and tone should be. And if I don't like it when I see it, I change it. And if the actor comes to me and says, I'm having a problem, how do you see this? I address it as whatever it is.

But as a director, one of the things that I always try and do is I'm always there before we're on the set. So if it's a 7 o'clock shooting call, I'm probably there by 5.30 or 6 o'clock because I want to talk to the actors when they're in makeup and hair. We have a chance to talk a little bit about what their thoughts might be about their part.

If they have any ideas or anything they don't understand or if I have an idea and I want to give it to them and it's just a moment of quiet where you can sit and talk to your artists about, and your actors, how you think you should play the scene. And for example, an actor may say, you know, there's 2 1⁄2 pages of dialogue in here and I have one line. I'm just standing there.

There's really no reason for me to be there except to deliver this one line. And the only line I have to hear is this line that motivates my line. What am I supposed to do? I go, that's easy.

I'm going to have a coffee set up there and you go and say, anybody want a cup of coffee? Everybody will nod and say no and you're going to go over and mix yourself a cup of coffee. It takes you out of the scene. So I fix stuff all the time.

I always said a director's a fixer. You're always doing those kind of things. But directing came naturally to me. I guess being boss is easier than doing the work. But you are the storyteller with a camera. You play everybody's parts.

You try and break a scene down because they're not made in continuity. You break a scene down in your mind. The homework for a director is what is the specific reason for this scene? What is the exposition that's being passed or what are we showing the audience? What's the story point of this scene? And then the next thing, if I was teaching a directing class back then, because I retired in 97, I would be saying, what's the first image you want the audience to see and what's the last image you want the audience to see that's leading to the next scene? And that's kind of a basic kind of philosophy I had as a director.

If I was talking to a class of future directors, I would be saying, what's the first image you want to see and what's the last image you want your audience to see? And I talked again about breaking down scenes, what the point scenes were. You're just a storyteller with a camera and your editor almost doesn't have to read the script notes coming in because he's looking at the film, he or she, and they are understanding exactly how you wanted to tell the story of that particular scene. Now, your job as director, let's just say we have a dining room scene, it's gotta have a purpose, right? Is it about tension? Laughter? Maybe something gets revealed. That determines everything – the lighting, the music, the actors' expressions – even what kind of flowers you have on the table, maybe. Details matter!

Anyways, a lot of exposition in that dining room scene, a lot of talking heads... problem is, the audience will tune out if you just shoot the script as is. They start to get bored. So, you get creative. Get someone up to pour a drink, have them fidget with something... something to keep the audience interested, otherwise they switch off.

Speaking of fidgeting... there was this time I was shooting a scene for McCloud. Two guys in an office, all talk, all business. I knew it was gonna be a snoozefest on screen, so I had this idea – gave one of the actors a squeaky chair. Every time he shifted, the squeaks made the other guy jump a little. The tension grew without a word of dialogue being changed! Sometimes, it's the little things that make the biggest difference.

Now, people often ask if I met my wife on the job. Nope, we were together long before either of us got into the business. Just in case you were wondering! See, being a director, I got to work with some living legends – guys like Howard Hawks, Billy Wilder... different styles, but they both knew how to tell a story.

Billy Wilder, he wrote everything he directed, so his films had that real personal touch. And hey, do you remember The Apartment? I was an apprentice on that one –

black and white, no color. That was Wilder's vision. Shadows were important to him, and he worked with this cinematographer, Joe LaShelle – brilliant guy.

Hawks was a whole different animal. There was always bits in his movies that reminded you of other stuff he had made. Like that "how do you like to kiss" scene, he used variations on that in a few movies. You knew it was a Hawks picture, even without reading the credits.

He had a different way of working, and a different kind of cinematographer he liked. Softer lighting, warm tones in the center... two amazing storytellers, both of 'em, just with their own ways of doing things. Hawks, he loved a challenge. There was this one scene in El Dorado, a big saloon brawl, a complete and total mess on paper. Hawks breaks it down, decides to shoot it almost entirely in slow motion, except for John Wayne. Made the mayhem crystal clear, and somehow, hilarious. Genius, that's what that man was.

See, people ask me what it takes to be a director. Truthfully, I don't know. If I can do it, anyone can! It's just about telling a story with pictures instead of words, right? Some stories you like more than others, that's all. I always liked making films, turning that stack of paper with words on it into something real, something that moves people. There's something magical about that, you know? The possibilities are endless. But I guess you always remember your first love – even though I've made a zillion movies, part of my heart is still behind the wheel of a race car.

In the beginning, I was fascinated by the whole thing. How this stack of paper, a script, could turn into something you see on the big screen... It seemed like magic! But after a while, a long while, it becomes... well, a job like any other. I think I reached a point where I'd just done it enough. That's the truth of it.

I used to ask my managers, how many of these darn movies do I gotta make before I can retire? They'd always say they'd let me know when the time was right. Then, of course, my heart starts acting up in the middle of hiatus – perfect timing, if you ask me. I call those managers, and boom, they're all, "Sure, take it easy! You've earned it." Funny how that works.

I wrapped up my commitments that year, and never looked back. Well, mostly. I did a couple of documentaries later on – that one about the Atlantic Rally, remember? And the yacht club anniversary... not exactly blockbusters, but they kept me busy. I always liked being behind the camera, even if the projects were smaller.

So, you want to hear a juicy disaster story, huh? Everyone loves to hear about that stuff! Honestly though, the worst problems usually come from some actor who's being a pain. Doesn't wanna work, doesn't like the lines... you're standing there on set, dozens of people waiting on your word, and the star decides to throw a temper tantrum. Those are the worst days, let me tell you.

Doesn't help that it happens more often than you'd think. Some actors, they just make your life difficult. I ain't naming names, but you get the picture. That's just part of the job, unfortunately. And I say job, because filmmaking really is just that – a job. Creative, maybe, but it's still work. Sometimes, it feels like less 'visionary artist' and more 'glorified babysitter', you know?

Thing you learn early on as a director is, never assume anything. Just because you think something should be done a certain way, doesn't mean your crew gets it. You gotta spell it out, check that it was done right, and check again. You gotta be there, all the time, or everything will fall apart. Remember my buddy Jack Arnold? Used to direct all those classic sci-fi movies back in the day? He taught me that lesson when I was still a newbie. Never forgot it.

There's an old saying, I think, about assumptions... something being the mother of all screw-ups? Well, it's true in Hollywood, that's for sure. Thing is, I never saw directing as a glamorous gig. It was fixing problems, getting the stars out of their trailers, making sure the set carpenter didn't use the wrong kind of wood... not exactly what they teach you in film school!

Let me give you an example. There was this one movie I did, won't name names, but big Western. Star of the show was this up-and-coming actor, talented, but a bit of a hothead. One day, we're ready to shoot this huge brawl scene, got the stuntmen wired up, the extras in place... and he just refuses. Says the dialogue's all wrong, wants a rewrite on the spot. Cost us half a day, but you gotta learn to roll with it in this business.

But yeah, I always say, being a director – you're half field marshal, half child psychiatrist. One half of you is trying to move an army, and the other half of you is trying to get people to do what you want them to do. That's the child psychiatrist part. That's my best description of a director.

Navigating Uncharted Waters: From Director's Chair to Captain's Helm

Now, you know I retired from directing years ago, but that gave me more time for my other passion... boats. See, I grew up in Seattle, surrounded by water. Boats everywhere, big, small, didn't matter. Any kid near the water is gonna fish, right? Hand-lines, dough balls for bait... whatever would bite. Been a fisherman all my life, drawn to the water.

We had this summer place on Vashon Island, and anyone visiting my folks with a decent boat, I'd sweet-talk them into letting me ride back to Seattle. My poor Dad, he'd have to take the ferry to get me... but, hey, it was worth it to be on the water. Ocean's been a huge part of my life. It's that feeling, you know? Getting on a boat, leaving land behind... even if it's just to find a good fishing spot.

Being a fishing captain, it's like being a guide. Gotta know where the fish are, help your clients hook 'em, keep what they want, release the rest... I've spent a good part of my life out there on the water. And I'll admit, I couldn't have done most of it without my wife. Funny, actually, she swore off men who owned boats when we met! Her ex-husband, they had one, and she was stuck doing all the maintenance. Tended to get a touch seasick too, bless her heart... but, luckily for me, she changed her mind!

That brings me to my boating legacy, as I call it. I'm the first guy to circumnavigate the world in a powerboat. Basically, you just need a boat with enough fuel to cross an ocean. Mine was this Delta, originally built as a commercial crabber – 70 feet long, held 4,000 gallons of fuel. My longest crossing was to Hawaii – 2,250 miles. Managed that, I could go pretty much anywhere.

Averaged a gallon a mile, ended up with about 2,000 gallons to spare. Cruised at about 8 knots, one generator humming all the time... maybe I'm getting too technical here, but this was an adventure! Started the whole thing back in... '89, I think? Ended up taking three years, right around early '91.

Took three years out of my life when I was on the director A-list. My agents were furious, said Hollywood doesn't care about my little hobby. Threatened me, said I'd never work again... well, turns out I was successful enough to take the risk. Both my mom and Joan's dad had passed away, so it felt like the right time. And the funniest thing – the day I'm literally stepping off the boat, my agents are there at the airport, hiring me to fix some botched pilot! Guess it all worked out in the end.

But why Australia, you ask? Well, that was my dream. Fish those waters, catch those giant marlin I'd heard so much about. Figured on running my own boat for the season, then shipping everything home. But while I was waiting for my boat to get picked up... well, let's just say, plans changed, and the circumnavigation happened kind of by accident.

Funny story, that – got approached by this film crew, wanted to document the whole journey across the Pacific. First, I said no, didn't want the attention. But the more I thought about it... well, if it helped pay for the rest of the trip, why not? They filmed me fishing in Australia, island hopping, crossing the Indian Ocean... the whole nine yards. Turned out to be a pretty popular documentary when it aired! Helped make the trip a reality, and put me in the record books.

See, when I took my boat to Australia, I had zero plans to go around the whole darn world. But things have a funny way of snowballing, wouldn't you say? There was a shipping strike, and then the first Gulf War kicked off...suddenly, my original route through the Suez was blocked. My insurance was canceled – too afraid of those poorly-controlled Scud missiles! That's when I got the idea to head for New Zealand instead. See, they weren't worried about Scuds down there, and the fishing was supposed to be pretty spectacular.

So, I spent a great season off New Zealand, decided to give Australia another shot the next year... and before I knew it, I was heading north to Darwin. Figured I could find a ship to pick up my boat in Singapore, but by the time I got there, the paint was looking a bit shabby. Now, back then, getting a boat that size properly repainted in Southeast Asia was a pain. But Fort Lauderdale? They had those huge sheds, Cuban crews who knew their stuff... so I figured, why not? That's when I added the detour via Bermuda into the plan.

Turns out, by the time I reached Bermuda, I had technically circumnavigated the world! I'd been there before, see, so crossing into the Atlantic again meant I'd been around the entire globe. Suddenly, I'm being told I'm the first to do the whole thing in a powerboat! Who'd have thought? So, I took the boat down to Florida, got it repainted, sailed through the Panama Canal, and was back home by Labor Day.

Pulled into Cat Harbor with all my flags flying – got a great picture of that in my office, all the countries I'd visited. Came into Marina Del Rey to fireboats and a full-blown celebration... suddenly I'm this boating celebrity. The whole thing was more than a bit surreal! But I'll tell you, I'm so glad I did it then, and my wife even more so. Times change, you know.

See, piracy wasn't the problem it is today. With all that's going on in the world, it would be impossible to replicate the trip safely now. My wife always says it was the trip of a lifetime. And looking back, she's right – perfect timing, perfect everything. Couldn't have asked for better luck, especially with how the war in the Gulf messed up my original plans!

Now, you're probably wondering how long the trip took. Well, I had set aside three years for it, and I was determined to finish what I started. True, I didn't get to see quite everything I had on my original itinerary... Missed out on England and some of the Mediterranean. I had to detour south via Singapore and Indonesia instead of the Suez, but it was an incredible adventure all the same.

There were places where a boat like mine was a downright novelty. Locals would stare, asking what in the heck this thing was and how it got there. I even had paperwork – got another great picture of that – making my boat look all official, like a research vessel studying Western tuna... added a touch of legitimacy, and definitely helped throw off some port officials. It opened some doors that might have stayed closed otherwise!

Usually had a crew of four, me, Joan, and a couple of deckhands. There were a couple ocean crossings where it was just us, and boy, those could get intense! Those were the days I really learned to respect the ocean, let me tell you. But let me tell you, my little green boat, she was a star! Made the cover of Yachting magazine twice in the same year – and back then, they were all about sailboats. Even got featured in their calendar, the only powerboat amongst the sailboats. Still a source of pride for me. We did something incredible, and it made an impact no one expected.

We pioneered something that's completely commonplace now – it's called weather routing. See, back in those days, this was before satellites and all the high-tech stuff. Somehow, we caught wind of this experiment Bendix was doing. They'd assembled a whole team of meteorologists down in Fort Lauderdale – some project about predicting wind patterns, and it turns out those racing sailboat guys were tapping into it during transatlantic races. Well, I got to thinking, if they can find wind, they can find calm, right?

My buddy Milt Baker, who co-owned Blue Water Books and Charts at the time, set up a meeting with the Bendix people. So there I am, asking these weather experts to predict storms for me as well as good sailing conditions. They seemed up for the challenge! Remember, there was no such thing as weather routing for pleasure boats, just for commercial airlines and shipping... and even then, they didn't use NOAA! They all had their own in-house weather guys, because the ones who built the best models had the best routes.

Now, back then, predicting weather was tough. Not as many sources as today. The very first satellite had just gone up, and nobody thought it would be much use over the Pacific, where I was headed. But we got creative – the Bendix guys needed weather reports from wherever we were sailing. My end of the bargain was giving them my coordinates and what I was seeing out on the water. In return, they'd build a model, radio their predictions, and we'd plot our course. They even got in touch with ham radio operators to help us stay in communication. Talk about teamwork, between our team, the meteorologists, ham radio guys... it was a real group effort! We were practically inventing weather routing for pleasure boats on the fly, and it started a whole new industry.

Oh, and speaking of being on the cutting edge... wouldn't you know it, we stumbled upon an early version of email! We called it Standard C. Had this little computer rig on the boat – didn't have a clue about computers back then, mind you – and a printer. Turns out, for it to work, we had to fax, yes fax, our messages to someone in Virginia! They'd feed them into the computer, and then it would eventually reach whoever it was meant for. Same thing going the other way. Amazing it even worked at all!

Funny thing, sometimes I'd get messages from our meteorologists asking me to tell other boats to type their faxes – they couldn't read the handwriting! Can you imagine trying to explain email and computers over a ham radio to a sailboat out there in the Pacific? They must have thought we were pulling their legs.

But hey, we had that one satellite, and that gave us an edge. We were getting weather reports when most other boats were still at the mercy of the wind and the waves. I loved working with those meteorologists. We were doing things that hadn't been done before, charting our own path. There was a real sense of camaraderie – and of course, the thrill of the unknown. I always say, I was lucky with my timing, being out there on the water just as all these technologies started to come together.

Nowadays, weather routing, email, satellites... none of that feels groundbreaking. Boaters check the weather on their smartphones, they've got fancy GPS systems, the routes are already mapped out. I miss the sense of adventure sometimes, you know? The world of boating is a whole lot different now, but I wouldn't trade those years of exploration for anything.

Crossing Oceans: The Birth of a Docudrama

My long history with boats put me in touch with a company called Nordhavn. They'd started out making sailboats, then kind of stumbled into long-range trawlers... and boy, did those catch on! They got this 46-footer Jeff Leishman had designed, and suddenly they were in a whole different market. I was a regular around their docks, sharing my years of experience to help them improve their designs. Then one day, Jim Leishman, their VP, calls me up with a proposition.

Turns out, they wanted to organize a massive Atlantic rally, a demonstration of what Nordhavns could handle. Just for their boats at first, but they needed help, someone with experience who could make it all go smoothly. I'd just retired, figured why not, so I said yes... but I had my own ideas. See, I told Jim, let's not limit this to Nordhavns, even though those were the majority of the boats at that point. Not a lot of other companies were building for transatlantic journeys back then. We could be the pioneers, showing the world what was possible! I figured out the logistics – stages based on boat speed and fuel capacity, so everyone felt safe and included.

Jim was on board, basically gave me free rein! My next step was to assemble the 'brain trust'. First, I got Milt Baker involved. He's an ex-Navy man, ran Blue Water Books and Charts before he sold it, and let me tell you, the Navy teaches you organization like nothing else. Perfect for setting up those land-based operations during our stopovers. Then I snagged this buddy of mine, a retired destroyer captain who'd just been made Admiral in the Gulf War. This guy knew the technical aspects of command inside and out! That's what I needed, a team who could cover all bases.

I mapped out the route, planned the support, all of it. And then – twist number one: Jim tells me we gotta make a documentary! Now, that sounded fun, but I went to these professional crews, and they wanted a two-man team on each boat. These trawlers aren't cruise ships, you know? That would mean cabin fever and a sky-high price tag. That's when I had that flash of inspiration – what if we did it ourselves?

Long story short, we ended up buying cameras directly from a manufacturer who gave us a great discount on slightly older models. Turns out, we were right on time with this whole thing, because it was over 10 years ago, and not everyone had a decent camera back then. We did a survey of our participants – had a whopping 36 boats at that point – and wouldn't you know it, half of them weren't equipped to shoot a proper video!

Now, chaos could have ensued, but luckily, I'd prepared for that. We bought cameras on their behalf, then hired this pro to give everyone a crash course. Turns out, even folks with the high-end gear weren't sure how to use them past the basics! And then – twist number two: a month before departure, 18 boats drop out! Talk about a planning nightmare, but hey, the ocean throws curveballs for a living, right? We rallied, pulled it together, and made it a learning experience. I realized that day, sometimes when you're out there leading an adventure, it's not just about the itinerary, it's about improvising, embracing the chaos, and finding the right people who'll weather the storm alongside you.

Teaching a bunch of first-time videographers how to make a scene was, let's just say, an eye-opener. Turns out, when things get exciting out there on the water – something breaks, a fish takes the bait – those cameras did more filming of people's butts than dramatic close-ups. You'd think with all the action, they'd have a knack for it, but no! I'd end up back on dry land, having to reassemble the best bits and pieces of what they shot.

Get the guy to put on the same shirt, climb back down into the bilge with them, do the whole thing again as a restage, just to get some decent shots! I got a crash course in movie editing, let me tell you. All because these folks couldn't decide if they were making a feature film or accidentally auditioning for America's Funniest Home Videos with all the unintentional slapstick. But hey, gotta work with what you've got out on the ocean, right?

But seriously, imagine trying to tell a story of this incredible rally if all your footage is just one guy struggling with a fishing reel for 20 minutes straight. Who the heck would watch that? I'd have to splice in stuff – line whizzing off the reel, close-up of the rod bending, the look on the poor guy's face... you wouldn't believe how meticulous we got! I mean, I wasn't calling it a documentary for nothing, but let's be real, it turned into a bit of a docudrama. Still, I traveled with them, met them at every stop, made sure that footage was at least somewhat usable.

And you should ask Nordhavn for a copy! They'll send it to you, free of charge, won't even make you pay shipping! It's an interesting watch if you're into boats. Though, fair warning, it's longer than I would have liked... 115 minutes. Like I always say, gotta learn to cut stuff out! Funny thing, it would have been shorter if we'd had time to do a proper voiceover... which takes me to a hilarious story.

See, I get the first rough cut done, and as a placeholder, I have my buddy Joe Swirling read the script. This was before syncing it to the film, just to help with editing the story. He's got this booming, friendly voice, figured it would be a nice temporary solution. Anyway, wouldn't you know it, Trawler Fest calls, wants the film to be the main event at their big dinner!

Now, I had to show the rough cut to the folks at Nordhavn before releasing it, in case something rubbed them the wrong way – corporate types, you never know what they'll get offended by, right? So, I fly out with the film, and they love it! They want to keep everything, even the parts where stuff's breaking and people are cursing! I had planned to put in a professional voiceover later, but they're all, 'No way, Joe's voice is perfect, leave it!'

I couldn't believe it! That's how my buddy Joe, with a temp track recorded in his garage, ended up narrating this whole massive boating rally documentary just because we were on a deadline. The film was a smash hit, of course, but that's showbiz for you, eh? It's all about improvising, making do with what you have, and sometimes, having a bit of dumb luck on your side doesn't hurt either!

You see, that final shot in Gibraltar, the one that ended up on a magazine cover, became a symbol of the whole journey. It sums up what these rallies are really about, doesn't it? Boats of all sizes, crossing an ocean together. But behind the scenes? Pure organized chaos! Trying to get eighteen skippers, each with their own way of doing things, to line up just right... I even had some yelling at me on the radio, questioning my sanity! You should have seen the looks on the Yachting Magazine crew's faces – they thought they'd hired a maniac. It's a good thing those things walkie-talkies weren't waterproof...

But here's the thing, we got the shot! And looking back at the film, the moments where some salty language spills out, or I'm losing my mind trying to get someone to adjust their course, those are some of my favorites. They aren't glamorous, that's for sure, but they're the true flavor of what it takes to make something like that happen. There's a real sense of camaraderie, the kind you only get when you're out there on the ocean and everything feels a bit... risky.

And do you know how I pulled off those end credits? I'll give you a hint: it involved some seriously creative reuse of existing footage. You've gotta get inventive when you're editing a docudrama that was basically shot on the fly! But here's the real secret, there was absolutely no way I could have done it alone. Joan was my rock the whole time. Tagging shots, describing the weather conditions, boat positions... it was a massive undertaking just keeping track of everything we filmed. I'm telling you, if she hadn't been there organizing the chaos, I'd probably still be staring at a mountain of raw footage. That's the power of having someone who understands your vision and is willing to sweat alongside you, even when it's not glamorous.

We didn't just film a rally, we captured a community. People still tell me that documentary inspired them to take the plunge, do their own crossing. And yes, you need the technical stuff, the shots of boats cutting through waves... but it's the moments in between, the human element, that make it truly compelling. That's why I get a little sentimental sometimes when those Nordhavn executives dig it up – because that film is as much a tribute to the team that helped me make it as it is to the ocean itself.

Filmmaking – whether it's a blockbuster thriller or a documentary shot at sea – it's a collaborative effort. The best directors get that. Sure, you have your vision, but if you don't have good people around you, the vision stays stuck in your head. That's what happened with The Sound of Speed, and so many other films I've worked on. An editor who sees the unspoken story in the footage, a composer who knows just the right notes to make your heart pound... those contributions are priceless.

Thing is, you have to be willing to listen, even when someone tells you the thing you poured your heart into just isn't working. Sometimes they're right. Sometimes the magic happens when you take their idea and put your own spin on it. And sometimes, even the outtakes are worth keeping. They may not make the final cut, but they're reminders of what you accomplished... and what you'll do differently next time!

The Cuban Grand Prix: A Race Like No Other

You've got to hear this... the Grand Prix of Cuba. If some writer pitched this to me as a movie idea, I'd roll my eyes, thinking they'd been watching too many cheesy B-movies. Kidnappings, champion drivers, the works... but I swear on my toolbox, it all went down! Picture this: Cuba, 1958. I'm fresh off a road trip from Connecticut, ready to burn rubber for Ferrari. My teammates? Come on... Phil Hill, Stirling Moss, Wolfgang von Trips... we're talking legends here.

Now, on the other side of the pits, Maserati rolls out their own all-star cast: Juan Manuel Fangio, the freaking world champion, Carroll Shelby... and hey, even I can't remember all the stars lined up to race! Just imagine the egos in those garages, thicker than the tropical humidity! And the track? Forget those fancy circuits. We're blazing through Havana's backstreets, then screaming around the Malecon, that waterfront boulevard... like a tropical Monaco, but with ten times the chaos.

Now, Ferrari, being Ferrari, doesn't exactly put us up at the Ritz. Nope, we're stuck in some local garage. Picture grease monkeys and dented fenders all around. And guess who my neighbor in the next stall is? Some rich South American playboy with a Testarossa. Wouldn't shut up, yapping away in English about this morbidly hilarious accident at an earlier race, someone getting killed. At first, I assume it's just dark racing humor, right? WRONG.

One of these guys, he's LAUGHING about it! Blasting the other driver for plowing straight into an outhouse, on the first lap no less! Can't believe some moron parked himself in an outhouse at the start of a race! Meanwhile, my stomach is turning. Turns out, the guy telling the story is the one who freaking KILLED SOMEONE! And he's passing it off as a joke! Right then and there, I realized these rich South American playboy racers – whole different breed, different set of rules. And probably not the best people to be sharing a track with...

Before long, I'm itching to find Fangio. I mean, I've seen the guy blaze past me, but I wanted a moment with the legend. I track down the Maserati garages, but day after day, he's mysteriously 'unavailable'. One day, I decide to try again, and what do I hear? Giggling girls! Yeah, turns out our beloved world champion was upstairs 'entertaining' a fan club the whole damn time! No wonder he couldn't spare a minute for a nobody like me. But let me tell you, during practice, that guy's skill... you wouldn't believe how he could manhandle a four-and-a-half-liter Ferrari. Turns out, true racing talent – and maybe a few Cuban ladies on the side – really can make you unstoppable.

Anyways, I'll tell you all about how the actual race ended later – because let me tell you, that's a whole different kind of crazy! But one thing's for sure: the Grand Prix of Cuba wasn't just a race. It was a wild peek behind-the-scenes, where drivers were either heroes or villains, the track was barely controlled chaos, and the stakes were beyond anything I'd ever imagined.

Let me tell you, Fangio behind the wheel was a sight to see. Even on those narrow Havana streets, crammed up against the buildings, he was an artist with the steering wheel. Windows would fly open, crowds leaning out just to catch a glimpse, and he'd wave back like he was on parade! That was Juan Manuel Fangio: maestro, superstar, and a damn good driver.

After a few days in paradise, things took a dark turn. I'd heard the rumors – Fangio had been back at his hotel, signing autographs in the lobby like the gentleman he was, when these two goons waltz in with guns! They stick one in his side, intimidate the crowd, kidnap the world champion, and then vanish. Talk about bad publicity! Fangio missing, Cuba in chaos, headlines blaring... the whole world was watching this fiasco unfold.

See, back then, Cuba was run by Batista – dictator with a capital D. And wouldn't you know it, he was in business with none other than Meyer Lansky, head honcho of the Jewish mafia! Cuba back then was stunning, a tropical Vegas for the East Coast, filled with glitzy casinos and raunchy shows. We couldn't help having a good time, especially with Von Trips showing me the ropes. All that came crashing down once Fangio was kidnapped.

We were locked down, guards posted, the works. It felt like a movie gone horribly wrong, and I'm one of the supporting actors now! Speaking of bad movies... middle of the night, you'd hear a knock on your door. Jump up thinking, "The kidnappers are here for me!" and find two giggling Cuban girls sent by some of the jokester drivers! It was pure insanity. Kennedy lived next door, I'd try to play it cool while they were giggling, like... 'No, no, Luigi, totally fine here! Nobody's getting kidnapped...'

You get the picture, right? Things were absolutely unhinged. And THEN! Batista invites all the qualified drivers to a special breakfast. Thing is, for a race like this, if a country doesn't have a car or driver in the mix, they get to start one at the back anyway. Some kind of courtesy thing. Turns out, the only Cuban racing was this guy – I think he was Batista's personal limo driver! Someone found him an old two-liter Ferrari, and they were going to let him race, just to keep things polite.

Now, I'm all about racing, not politics. But that breakfast? Forget it. I couldn't stomach it, and neither could most of the other drivers. Found out later that nobody showed! So, what happens? They line up the cars, Batista's ready to wave the flag, drivers nowhere to be found... and what happens? He starts the race anyway! And that Cuban chauffeur, dead last, takes off with everyone else gone!

It's a great anecdote, right? But it gets even better from there, I promise. I'll tell you about how the race actually went down, and how the Fangio situation unfolded. It's a good reminder – truth really can be stranger than fiction, especially when racing, dictators, and the mafia are all involved!

We're roasting inside those cars, lined up on the sweltering starting grid, the roar of the crowd pressing in from all sides. It's already a recipe for disaster. Then it happens – "Get in the cars!" We're in, sweaty, hands shaking. Then... "Start your engines!" The thunder of the V12s explodes, the cars vibrating with barely contained power. We're ready to RACE... and then nothing.

We're just sitting there, idling for what feels like hours, the heat becoming unbearable. Drivers are getting restless, the tension thickening with every passing second. And then, Phil Hill shuts down his engine. Calm as can be, he climbs out of the Ferrari and just walks away! Like he's going to catch up on his reading, not about to get heatstroke in this circus of a race.

It's contagious, like a ripple effect. All these big-name drivers, Moss, Shelby, me... we're shutting down our engines, spilling out of the cars, joining this bizarre little protest right there on the starting grid. And those thousands of fans, they're looking at us like we've lost our minds. Honestly, we probably had. Talk about a photo op! I still have a vision of Tim Considine scrambling with his camera – those images probably ended up in some racing history book, that moment of defiance at the Cuban Grand Prix.

Then, just like that, complete panic. "Get back in! The race is starting!" We're scrambling, engines roaring, the green flag drops, and it's instantly a mad scramble. Now, remember, those cute stoplights lining the streets were doubling as race flags. So... a few laps in, I'm hitting the Malecon, the ocean breeze whipping past me, and those lights turn RED!

I slam on the brakes, cars piling up behind me, the noise of panicked engines bouncing off the buildings... what the heck is happening? None of us have a clue, nobody's told us anything. Then, I see the first car reverse course, turn around right on the track, and start heading back toward the pits – going the wrong way! Madness. Figured, when in Rome, right? If everyone else is bailing, I'm not going to be the idiot stuck on a battlefield.

Back in the pits, complete anarchy. Moss, he's hiding his fiance under a cover so she can escape... and I remember hearing later he made a beeline for the airport. Me? I'm still reeling from those gunshots ringing out earlier. I don't even see a race official anywhere, just chaos and confusion. Turns out, that Cuban driver they'd given a seat to as a favor? He'd spun into the crowd, people had rushed to help, and those military guys – they weren't aiming AT anyone specifically, their rifles blazed into the air to warn the crowd back, but it just added to the horror of the day.

No idea how many people ended up getting hurt or worse, but that was it... the race was done, just dead on the track. Fangio being released eventually, that's part of the larger story, but for me, those are the images of the Grand Prix of Cuba: Drivers on strike, red traffic lights, the chilling echo of gunfire... the day an international race turned into a full-blown disaster.

Moss is gone as soon as we realize what's happening, whisked away with his fiance to the airport, no idea what he's thinking. All of us drivers, meanwhile, we're herded into the sports palace, the whole team, and there's Kennedy standing there, looking cool as anything. Turns out, he had the starting money, the cash we were owed. He tells me they needed me to play courier – I'd fly to Miami, someone would meet me, and the money was safe. My head's spinning, thinking we'll probably be kidnapped next, maybe because of Fangio, maybe because of the race collapsing under Batista's nose... wouldn't that make a great Fourth of July celebration for him, right?

But then, out of nowhere, the biggest surprise yet. Uproar, voices raised...and who strolls in but Juan Manuel Fangio, in the flesh! Turns out, they'd taken him some fancy estate, wined and dined him, the whole nine yards... until he basically told them, "Look fellas, great party, excellent food, but this is starting to reflect poorly on my reputation, so best I get on home." Turns out, Castro's whole goal was to embarrass Batista, prove his government was weak... and they did it with fine wine, good food, and maybe even a few pretty girls!

And me? I'm on a flight back, gripping that briefcase of cash, thinking every minute someone's going to try to rob me. But no! Guy in Miami takes the cash, polite as you please. And that, my friends, is the Cuban Grand Prix – a total fiasco, a clusterf*** of epic proportions, and a story that never really made it out there the way it should have. You couldn't make this stuff up if you tried.

Speaking of insane schemes, while all this was happening, Ronnie Burns – George Burns' son, my roomy in Hollywood at the time – calls. Says Rod Amato, the director of the Burns and Allen TV show, is chartering a plane to come rescue me! I had to put a stop to that real quick – bad enough the whole world was watching this fiasco, I didn't need a film crew documenting my rescue too!

Funny how that whole mess prepared me for even grander adventures. Remember FUBAR? The San Diego to La Paz boat rally I launched? Nobody had organized anything like that before, they thought I was nuts. But the Cuban Grand Prix taught me two things: you've got to embrace the chaos, and there's always an opportunity to raise some money for a good cause, no matter how ridiculous things get. Turns out, even cancelled races can lead to the best stories... and the greatest challenges!

I'll tell you, I spent a lot of time after that lobbying the US government to let us take powerboats to Cuba. Think about it: all those beautiful harbors, that tropical water... a boater's paradise that was off-limits because of politics. Finally, after years of red tape and negotiations, we managed to pull it off! A whole fleet of boats, US government approval... a huge step forward. Of course, it would have been even easier if they had let us race there back in the '50s, but hey, that's history for you, right?

Now, imagine trying to explain all this to the average person. They'd think I was pulling their leg – the world champion kidnapped, a race called off after a few laps, a protest on the starting grid, gunshots echoing in the street... it's like a rejected Coen brothers movie script, right?

But that was Cuba under Batista: beautiful, corrupt, absurd, and always, ALWAYS dangerous. After Fangio strolled out of the jungle looking like he'd been at a resort, everyone scattered. The whole place was on lockdown, the race an embarrassment that Batista wanted erased as quickly as possible. We barely got out of there alive, but I'll tell you, the stories stuck with me.

Funny, though, that wasn't even the last time I'd find myself tangling with Caribbean dictators. Years later, with FUBAR a hit, I got this idea ... what if I could convince the U.S. government to let us, a group of American powerboaters just eager to explore, sail to Cuba? See, after Fangio, I had this itch. Cuba was right there, practically begging to be explored by boat, and it was off-limits. That just didn't seem right.

So, I started lobbying. Bureaucrats, senators, anyone I could get a meeting with. They all thought I was nuts, of course. It was illegal to go there, never mind the tension between Washington and Havana – but what did they know about adventure? It was a long, uphill battle, but you know, that Cuban Grand Prix taught me two things: never give up on a crazy idea, and always be prepared for the unexpected.

Finally, the day came – we got the official seal of approval. A whole fleet of American boats setting sail for Cuba, a first in who knows how long. It wasn't the high-speed thrills of a Grand Prix, but man, there's something about approaching those shores with the government's blessing... It was a different kind of victory, maybe even sweeter because it meant we weren't the pawns in someone else's political game.

Looking back, though, I think those early days racing cars and dodging bullets in Havana, those were formative experiences in a way. I learned that life isn't about sticking to the script, it's about improvising when the plan goes sideways, and about finding opportunity even in the heart of chaos. And if a story like the Cuban Grand Prix isn't proof of that, I don't know what is. I'd give anything to go back in time and slap a camera on Fangio's kidnappers – now THAT, my friends, would be a movie worth watching.

A Historic Voyage: The First U.S. Authorized Fleet to Cuba

Okay, you know those moments when it feels like the whole world has lost its mind? Well, that was me, trying to organize a charity boat trip to Cuba as a way to get around all the political red tape. Boating magazines loved the idea, thought my experience with FUBAR would be the key, and it took four years (yes, four!) to get those bureaucrats in D.C. to budge. Obama eased travel restrictions, and suddenly, it's ON! They call me up, give me about three weeks to get everything organized, like these events pop up overnight, right?

So, I round up a decent posse of boats at Key West, and get ready for the crossing. Now, beforehand, I ask these multi-millionaires on their shiny sport fishing boats, those they call 'warships', if any of them even know how to get to Cuba. Turns out, they haven't a clue. Their captains do the thinking, and apparently, NONE of them have been down there either. I tell them, "Hey fellas, you get to Customs, you tip $10,

MAX. That's standard." Wouldn't you know, first boat pulls in, the captain marches up to me, furious. Wants $1,000 back. Apparently, Cuban officials shake him down, and his owner caved and paid up! I just look at him, dead serious, and say "Captain, you should know better. I warned you guys, didn't I?" That $1,000? Gone. Lesson learned the hard way.

We finally get to Havana, and I check into the hotel. Joan, my wife, and a friend have been down there earlier, taking photos and getting the lay of the land. Picture this: Room's $40 a night, unlimited drinks and food, 24-7. This was before Cuba became a tourist hotspot, so prices were practically out of a time warp. I decide to treat everyone who came down with me, so we gather at the hotel bar. I'm playing the gracious host, buying rounds of drinks ... then go to pay the tab. Bartender looks at me, stumped. Why? Because they have no system for billing drinks to a room! We laugh it off, and head down the street to the Havana Yacht Club.

It smells amazing, they've got a whole roasted pig going, the works. We settle in, people order lobster, steaks, whatever their hearts desire, then finish it off with fancy desserts. When the bill comes, for a group of 13 after all that? It averages about $13 per person! Seriously, try finding that kind of deal back home. You realize that while Cuba has its issues, there's this unspoiled charm to it, this throwback quality that's both frustrating and refreshing.

But here's the best part, right? Captain Eskridge of the Cuban sailing team, the guy we were doing this all for? He's so grateful for the boats we donated, it's heartwarming. We've made a real connection, and I feel like it's starting to pay off, all those years pushing for this. See, it's not just about the racing, the adventure. Sometimes, it's about proving you can get things done, no matter how many times they tell you it's impossible. And hey, who wouldn't want to be the guy who helped get more boats into Cuban waters, right?

Now, about those Optis... honestly, without a sail, they're about as exciting as a bathtub! Masts down, nestled on the decks, they probably looked more like oversized dinghies to those Cuban Customs guys. Which was a stroke of luck, because back then they had this strict 'no gifting' policy. Think of it this way: they didn't want folks coming in and then leaving behind their old junk just because they got tired of hauling it back to the US! No donating your faded Miami Dolphins T-shirt or leaving that chipped baseball bat just because it took up space.

It took a little creative thinking. See, that's the thing about dealing with bureaucracy – sometimes you've gotta be smarter than the system, find loopholes those rigid pencil-pushers never planned for. So I cornered the Commodore, a sharp guy, luckily with an even sharper assistant to translate everything. "Listen," I tell him, "I'm gonna 'loan' you those boats. And by loan, I mean don't expect 'em back for a good long while!" We whip up some paperwork right there in the office, making it nice and official. Those sailboats were officially on indefinite loan to the Cuban junior racing team! Chances are, if you visit Havana's yacht club today, you'll see some kid out there zipping across the water in one those little boats we brought along. Hey, sometimes a well-timed bit of wordplay is all it takes to navigate bureaucracy and leave something worthwhile behind.

Let me tell you, getting that fleet authorized though… that was a four-year fight against pure inertia! I could write a whole book just on dealing with those suits in Washington – half the time, I think they thought a sailboat was some kind of exotic bird, and had no clue why anyone would want to bring one down to Cuba. It was maddening! But the day Obama eased those travel restrictions, boy, did the tune change! Suddenly, I'm getting calls from the same guys who acted like I'd lost my mind, wanting the whole thing done yesterday! It's like they suddenly remembered boats existed, and assumed I could just snap my fingers and organize a whole darn regatta.

The news gets around about the trip, and sure enough, those Miami real estate bigwigs start to circle with their clients in tow. You know the type – they own those fancy sportfishing boats, the kind with more chrome and leather than a classic Cadillac, and suddenly they want IN on the action! But something about their whole attitude just rubs me wrong. "Look," I tell 'em, "tell your clients to pack a bag and be in Key West, and we'll see if there's room." Funny how most vanished when it turned out this wasn't a luxury cruise!

But the trip itself? Making history with that first authorized US fleet... let me tell you, it was worth every fight and every penny spent. I wrote about the whole thing for PassageMaker, "Havana on the Horizon", because those words felt bigger than just recounting the trip itself. It was proof that the tide was changing, proof that we were knocking down old barriers. And it wasn't just about the bragging rights, it was about sharing that feeling of accomplishment, proving that sometimes, you just gotta set sail and see where the winds of change will take you!

Speaking of changing tides... someone asked about Luigi Kennedy and good old NART, right? Well, Luigi was a force of nature, let me tell you! The heart of a lion, a head full of dreams, and let's just say his organizational style was... chaotic is a polite word! If you owned a race-ready prancing horse and Luigi had a race in mind, well, consider that car requisitioned! Now, he'd probably call you, make things right if you wrecked it, but let's just say it didn't always boost confidence before a big race! Hey, a guy's gotta do what he can to stay in the fight, right?

For us drivers, usually stuck with customers' cars, the real treat was those World Championship events like Sebring. That's when the factory stepped up with works cars, machines built to absolute perfection... let me tell you, it's a feeling unlike anything else when you get to pilot one of those marvels. But 1958, that's when the North American Racing Team really started to make its mark on the world stage. And me, Phil Hill, Dan Gurney... we were at the heart of it, laying the groundwork for what US professional racing would become. Yeah, we'd get handed a customer car sometimes, but it was belonging to that team, pushing yourself and your machine to the limits, knowing that win or lose, you're part of the most thrilling sport in history. And THAT feeling, my friend, is the real victory. It's a fire that never goes out, even after the checkered flag is waved, and every race has been run.

Racing Legends and the Dawn of Professionalism

The way cars were assigned back then... well, let's just say it wasn't exactly a meritocracy! Works cars, those marvels from the Ferrari factory, they'd usually go to Phil, our fearless leader. Meanwhile, guys like me and Dan Gurney, we'd end up with whatever customer car was handy. I can't tell you how many times they handed me the keys, and my heart sank a little. I never liked the cars I got! But hey, you gotta work with what you're given, and somehow I'd usually manage to cross the finish line.

That's where the thrill of those early NART years was, see. It was pushing yourself to the limit even in a machine that wasn't quite right, knowing it wasn't just for yourself - it was about setting the stage for what professional racing could become in America. Of course, we weren't above taking some money here and there! That Sebring prize... yeah, we might've been 'amateurs' technically, but getting paid to race felt pretty darn professional! Still, it wasn't until those guys at USAC took over Indianapolis, turned the whole racing scene into a proper business, that we officially became pros. That fall of '58, that was the turning point.

Suddenly, Kennedy was the big boss, assigning drivers like we were pieces on a chessboard. He'd even lend us out at will... the time he sent me to drive for John Edgar, well, that one still makes me laugh. But that's how it was back then – the drivers didn't call the shots, especially where Ferrari was concerned. We were at Kennedy's mercy, driving whatever he decided, and boy, were there some hilarious stories that came out of that…

I'll never forget that one race with NASA, driving Lance Reventlow's Maserati. Fastest qualifier, that little two-liter, but then the transmission started acting up. We had to withdraw, and I'm walking through the pits feeling dejected, when up strides Kennedy. "What happened to your car?" he demands. I explain about the transmission, that we're pulling it apart hoping to fix it, but that we're out for the day.

The man gives me this look, bellows "Grab your helmet, let's go!", and marches me straight over to some poor fashion photographer chap. This guy, he owns himself a brand-new Ferrari Monza, and he's all prepped to race. Well, Kennedy just taps him on the shoulder and says, "Get out." Dude tries to argue, points at his car... and Kennedy just huffs, "GET OUT!" The poor guy didn't stand a chance. One minute he's adjusting his driving gloves, the next I'm strapped in his seat and the flag is dropping!

Now, you gotta understand, this was a serious race, and Bobby Said? He was in it, driving light and nimble. But somehow, I managed to pull off the win in a car I'd never driven before. Afterwards, Bobby's throwing shade, complaining that it's a shame they let short guys race these powerful cars. Then someone tells him it wasn't the owner driving, and the guy goes, "Oh, Bruce? Yeah, well that's different…" That's just how it went. Kennedy ruled the roost, and if he decided you were racing something, well, you'd better be prepared to give it your best shot! The man had no fear, and sometimes, that led to some truly unforgettable moments.

Luigi Kennedy. Let's just say the man didn't mince words! "Get out," he'd tell some poor owner, and that was that – they'd be out of their car and I'd be strapped in before they could blink. It's chaos, but thrilling chaos! You never knew what you'd be driving on race day. Now, a factory-fresh Ferrari, now those were special... but they almost always went to Phil. Smart guy, Kennedy, putting his eggs in the winning basket. Me, yeah, if I had to rank myself, I'd probably have been considered third on the team, after Gurney.

Gurney... let's just say I think the hierarchy got to him a little. Remember the first US Grand Prix? He comes up to me, face like a thundercloud, complaining that his car's a dog. Phil's got a factory special, of course, Dan's got something decent, but he's not happy, and I'm already resigned to driving a lemon. Anyway, he spots my front tires, and wouldn't you know, they were the same size some guy – Moss, I think – ran when he won some NASA race.

He looks at me, all intense, and says, "Give me those tires." I shrug and say, "Sure, man, my car isn't doing anything anyway." Let's just say that didn't go over well with Phil... but hey, what did I care? Figured, at best, the swap might help Dan move up the ranks, at worst, my car wouldn't be any slower!

Race day arrives, and there's this misty drizzle. Transmission in the back, long gear lever... and wouldn't you know it, as the flag drops and everyone peels off, I'm convinced I've stalled the darn thing! Took my foot off the throttle, ready to call for a restart, and suddenly the car lurches forward. Those rain-slick tires somehow spun, but the tach got jammed on the wrong side... I'm picturing Luigi's furious face, thinking "How the heck do I explain this?!" as I start tearing through the pack!

Rain makes for unpredictable racing, that's for sure. Soon enough, I'm passing Phil – he spun out, and I had nowhere else to go! He eventually works his way back in front, but the track's a nightmare. Then, Phil drops out for some reason, and Bonnier with his F1 Maserati is sitting pretty at the front. Remember, this was a Formula Libre – anything goes kind of race, so I figure, might as well give it my best shot!

So, there we are, Gurney and I, chasing down Bonnier in that beast of an F1 Maserati, but we're not gaining any ground. Then, wouldn't you know it, I throw a tread on the backstretch. The car doesn't quite feel right, so I slow down for the next corner, and that's when it hits me – the tire's shaking the whole car! All this happening in the one race my dad decides to come watch from New York... what are the odds, right? As I pull into the pits, I see him standing there in his fancy cashmere coat, watching the crew scramble for the jack.

The poor guy, Bless his heart, he tries to help! I come in hot, spot him out of the corner of my eye, and he's grabbing another jack, thinking he's going to change the front tire! I almost ran him over in my haste to stomp on the brakes. Thankfully, someone tackled him just in time, and I got that tire changed.

Fast forward to the end of the race – I'm barreling across the finish line, and as I make the turn and start heading uphill, I spot Gurney. His car, that beautiful Nassau winner, is parked on the side of the road. He flags me over, looking sheepish as hell. Turns out, he wants a ride back to the pits! So I strap him to the car, somehow, and off we go.

Arriving back, I hear Phil yelling at me. "If only you had gone one more lap, you'd have gotten second!" I look at him, confused. "Phil, I DID finish second!" He explains that his engine blew right as he crossed the finish line, so he managed to coast all that way before coming to a stop. Well, wouldn't you know, that little detail put me in third!

Meanwhile, Kennedy is fuming. He's checking my tach, demanding to know how it ended up jammed on the wrong side. I try to explain about the tire mishap, but he's not having any of it. And on top of all that, Dan's engine is toast!

That night, over dinner – funded by splitting up the money from second and third place – my dad gets right down to business. He looks at Dan, all serious, and says "Dan, tell me, you have all those children... how do you afford to do this racing for a living?" Dan, ever the optimist, looks my dad straight in the eye and says, "Mr. Kessler, I promise, I'll figure it out! Don't worry, someday I'll find a way to make this whole racing thing pay the bills."

You gotta admire the guy's spirit, right? He just had this unshakeable belief in himself. My dad, well, he wasn't convinced, mostly worried about all those Gurney kids, but he always took an interest in Dan's career. Every time he read something in the paper or I filled him in, he'd ask, "How's your friend Dan doing?" It was sweet, even if he couldn't quite understand the appeal of this crazy sport. But hey, the heart of a dad is a funny thing, even when it comes to guys like us who were clearly more at home on the track than in the office!

Ol' Shelby, now there was a character straight outta some dime-store Western. Texan through and through, all hat and no cattle, like my pop would say. Always had that glint in his eye, like he knew a secret the rest of the world was too slow to catch onto. But hell, that big phony Texan could drive the wheels off a grocery cart.

Me, I started out driving for Tony Paravano. Didn't know much back then, just a young buck with more guts than sense. But Shelby took me under his wing, showed me the ropes. Taught me everything about wrangling a big engine, how to feel that power, not fight it. See, most folks, they think of Shelby and those Mustangs. And sure, the guy made an empire outta those cars, put his name on everything from chili mix to aftershave. But don't let that fool you. Above all, Carol Shelby was a racer.

Champion-grade racer. Won every dog-gone title there was, drove those little European sports cars like they were born mean. And those limeys in their Aston Martins? Yeah, they picked a chicken farmer from East Texas to drive their Formula One machine. That tells you somethin', right there.

Now, Shelby could be a handful. A regular Billy Sol Estes, that's what we used to call him, always hatching some new scheme, a sure-fire way to either make a fortune or land himself in the hospital. But he was my friend, see? We had some wild times, me and Carol.

Take that Tijuana road race – pure chaos from start to finish. Me in an old Corvette, Shelby in some borrowed jalopy that barely held together. Bandits, breakdowns, more dust than sense... but we made it, grinning like idiots. I could spin Shelby yarns all damn day.

Like that night at the Peterson, that gala they threw for me. Man of the hour, right? Well, Shelby was supposed to be the guest speaker. They'd told me he was stuck in the hospital, wasn't gonna make it. Everyone's giving me those sad-eyed looks 'cause Shelby's a no-show. But then I see him walkin' through the door, lookin' pale and a little unsteady, a nurse trailin' behind like he might make a run for it. Comes up to me and says, "Bruce, I couldn't miss this for the world."

So, there I am getting ready for my big moment at the Peterson Museum. Still feels a little strange, being the guy everyone's fussing over. Ol' Shelby shuffles up, still a bit pale from his latest hospital stay. You gotta give the man credit – even feeling under the weather, he never lost that mischievous grin. He looks me straight in the eye and says, "Bruce, I got just one favor to ask: keep that speech of yours short. Don't go chewin' the fat for hours, alright?"

See, that was pure Carol. Even when he's weak, gotta get that last jab in. But don't be fooled – under that Texas swagger, the man was a legend. One of the best damn drivers to ever come out of this country, and a lot of folks forget that. A magician behind the wheel, that Shelby.

And that man was my friend. I owe him more than a few beers, let me tell you. Remember back when Paravano was importing cars faster than you could say 'customs inspection'? Ferraris, Maseratis, you name it – the man had a whole fleet, changing them out like neckties. Shelby'd always grab the big, growling beasts, and I'd get the zippy little sports cars. We'd head out to Willow Springs, back when it was rougher than a dirt road brawl.

I'd wrap up my testing, and Shelby'd pull in, maybe in a hulking Maserati that sounded like a thunderstorm. You could just see it in his eyes, that itch to get back on the track. He'd give that grin and say, "Kessler, wanna take five with me? Might learn a thing or two." Those five laps, man... Shelby didn't preach, he didn't give no textbook lectures. He just drove, and I watched. The way he tamed those machines, smooth as silk but with more power than a runaway train...that shaved years off my learning curve. Yeah, when I moved up to the big-league cars, I owed a whole lot to Shelby. You didn't just learn from him, you felt it in your bones, that rhythm he had with the track. Just a damn good guy, under all the bluster. Y'know, most of the wild stories you hear about him? Probably dead true. Shelby was the kinda character that made racing twice as much fun to watch.

Speaking of wild, I'm pretty sure that man went through more hearts than a bad poker player. If I remember right, they swapped 'em out twice. That's why he hung up the helmet back in '58 or '59... heart trouble finally caught up to him, even with guts outsizing that Texas hat of his. But in his prime? Nobody – and I mean nobody – could touch Carroll Shelby behind the wheel. He was one of a kind, that's for damn sure.

From the Circuit to the Screen: Lessons a Driver Learned

So, Briggs Cunningham...didn't know him well. Wealthy guy, married this woman...Maxine Elmer was her name, at least back in the day. Ran in high-society circles, changed her first name to something fancy later on, can't remember it offhand. One of those society dames who'd make you feel like you had mud on your boots, even when you were all dressed to the nines. Met her once in New York with Briggs, had a connection through an old jazz musician she used to be married to.

Cunningham, now he knew my name, of course. But we weren't golf buddies or anything. Still, Maxine stuck with him 'til the end, bless her heart...not the prettiest gal, mind you. A bit rough around the edges, maybe took a few too many knocks before Briggs. But hey, some marriages, they just last.

After I hung up my helmet, didn't keep in touch with that crowd much. Shame about that Cunningham Museum though...heard they had one of Lance Reventlow's

Formula One cars, on top of whatever I donated. Thing is, I wouldn't even know what became of those cars. It's a funny thing about getting older, the way things fade...

Y'know, walking away from racing... that wasn't easy. One day you're getting offers from Maserati, the next...well, you're something else. Lance, he saw it. Kept sayin', "Bruce, time to move on". But to really quit, really leave that life behind, I had to cut the cord clean. Couldn't spend my days lookin' back, even if it meant turning down big races. That racing world, it gets in your blood.

And this new path of mine... well, it ain't the same. You miss the rush, the roar of the crowd. Miss being that guy, the one everyone's watching. Makes for good stories, though, and let me tell you, I got a whole bag full. But that's for another time, maybe...

Hell, life on the circuit was something else entirely. Royalty, con men, the whole damn circus rolled into one. The people you meet, the things you see...they don't make 'em like that in any other walk of life. Probably made me a better director in the end. Sometimes I'd change a scene, throw in some odd character... producers would give me that 'where'd that come from?' look. Came from my time on the road, that's where. The weird, the wonderful, the downright unbelievable...you find it all out there, with the oil stains and the champagne.

Maybe a circus would give you the same kind of view. But me? I had my ticket with those racing teams. Doubt I'd have traded it for anything...even if sometimes I wonder what might've been if I'd stayed behind the wheel just one more year.

Monte Carlo's got this way of making you feel small, even when you're hot off a win. All those fancy yachts, the champagne popping like gunfire...and me, I always preferred a burger and a Coke to that whole scene. Figured I'd grab a quiet bite before tackling qualifying, so I duck into one of those smoky little bars tucked away near the harbor. And that's when I see her…

This American girl, bright eyes and a smile that didn't quite belong in a place like that. She sat hunched over a drink next to some guy in flowing white robes, the kind that just scream "hidden weaponry". He gets up, maybe to use the restroom, and some instinct in me takes over. Maybe it was the boredom talking. Whatever it was, I found myself sliding into the empty chair, asking about the race, trying to make her laugh.

Didn't take long for trouble to find me. Another guy, sharp suit and sharper eyes, materializes at my elbow and hisses something about Arab princes and nasty habits. Turns out his wife's a fan of the circuit, and he fills me in while I try to process what just happened. Then, just when I think it can't get weirder, he pops the question: "Ever hunted tigers?"

Now, I'd taken down my share of game in the backwoods, but tigers? That's a whole different level. Still, something in his tone told me this wasn't a joke. When he mentions an all-expenses-paid trip to India, I start to see the whole thing play out like one of those pulp adventure stories I used to read as a kid.

Weeks later, I'm back in Beverly Hills, still feeling the California sun on my face. And in my hands? A fancy-schmancy invitation, like something out of a period drama. Now the doubts start creeping in. Is this some elaborate prank? A trap? I call the number, heart pounding a little too fast for my liking. A crisp voice on the other end assures me it's the real deal. Flights, guns, clothes – everything's covered, just bring a friend and a suitcase.

That's when I ring up Lance. My voice must've sounded off because even over the phone, I can feel him raise an eyebrow. "Tiger hunt," he drawls back. "Don't those fellas carry big rifles?" Makes a good point, doesn't he? I thank the mystery man, make my excuses, and hang up. Never even asked his name.

Left me wondering though...that's the thing about racing those years. The rush of the track, the champagne showers, sure...but it was the off-the-wall absurdity lurking in every corner that made it all so damn unforgettable. One minute you're dodging jealous princes in dimly-lit bars, the next you're fielding invitations to hunt with some nameless Indian Maharaja. Made you wonder if maybe life wasn't such a straight line after all, but one hell of a wild, unpredictable ride.

So, there I was, a young buck fresh off making The Sound of Speed, sweating it out at the Cannes Film Festival. Thing is, back then I mostly knew which end of a wrench to hold. Turns out, running in that crowd was a whole different kind of race. Alex Lucas – what a character, sadly no longer with us – his old man was a Hollywood shark with the fancy surname Lukachevitz. The kind of banker who shuffled millions, not spark plugs. Never knew a thing about that world 'til Alex dragged me along.

One minute I'm trying to figure out if my film even has a shot at some award, the next I'm chowing down at lunches with guys who owned half of Europe and probably a few scandals. To top it all off, I somehow ended up crashing at Zanuck's villa. Yeah, THE Richard Zanuck, Fox Studios big cheese even though he was nowhere to be found. Guess even movie moguls gotta take a vacation sometimes. Still, sleeping in a bed that probably cost more than a whole season of racing was a hell of a way to see how the other half lived.

See, that was the crazy thing about those years – life threw curveballs faster than the average track. Rubbing shoulders with the high and mighty, then getting your hands dirty under a car the next day, trying to squeeze another lap out of a busted engine. And those limeys, with their stiff upper lips and their currency restrictions…that's where I developed my knack for…shall we say, creative logistics.

See, back then, an Englishman couldn't take much of his own money outta the country. But me? With my American passport and regular hops back and forth to Italy for car stuff…well, let's just say my jeans started fitting a bit snug. Every bloke I knew after a race was giving me the side-eye, begging for some international assistance with their cash flow. That's how I earned my stripes as an amateur money smuggler – stacks of pound notes taped to my legs under two sets of denim. Necessity's the mother of invention, or so they say, and a young racer's gotta do what he can to stay in the game.

Speaking of the game, there was Rob Walker – top bloke, the one I drove Formula 2 for. Real gentleman of the old school, always had a kind word even when things went sideways. He was there that grim day when Mike Hawthorne left the road for the last time…tragedy like that leaves a lingering smell of burning oil, even on the toughest of us.

Anyway, Rob, he was always partial to a bit of scheming. Had this Cooper that wasn't doing much good, figured we'd sneak it down to Monaco, punch out the engine a bit, see if that little bugger didn't like the twisty streets. Plan was simple, at least on paper: stick an aging French driver, Trintignant, in the Cooper – good guy, on the downside of his career, but steady. He's there for insurance, to qualify in case my Connaught throws a fit. Well, wouldn't you know – my car conks out, and twelve cars slower than me didn't even make the race.

So there's Trintignant, stuck in that Cooper. The switching plan goes up in smoke as fast as my engine, but you know what? He not only qualifies, the old boy manages to out-smart, out-drive everyone, and wins the whole bloody Grand Prix! It was his final bow, too. Now, the whole paddock was alive with chatter…cars breaking down, smoke, drivers spinning out, the works. And on that track, the Cooper was the cat amongst pigeons. Left me wondering, of course, along with every other reporter in the pits. Could've, should've, would've…those questions stick with a racer long after the trophies are tarnished.

Part of me thinks I might've hung up my helmet right then and there if I'd pulled off a miracle win. But I was 22, hungry, maybe even a bit reckless. Those thoughts still gnaw sometimes…maybe that's where the 'what if' itch that every good director has took root. Nowadays, these Formula 1 kids are barely old enough to drive outta their momma's garage. Groomed from the crib, million-dollar teams, the whole shebang. Back then it was...scrappier. What a wild, head-spinning education it was. The wins, the losses, the near-arrests for smuggling cash, the long nights with half-empty champagne bottles and faces of guys I never saw again…it's not just racing lessons you pick up in a life like that. It shapes you, seeps into your bones, and when the roar of the engines finally fades, well…that's when it gets real interesting. That's where a movie director starts lurking, hungry for his next big story.